A Grand Tale

THE HISTORY OF **GRAND GENEVA RESORT & SPA**

ISBN: 978-0-615-83008-7

Grand Geneva Resort & Spa
7036 Grand Geneva Way
Lake Geneva, WI 53147
262-248-8811
www.grandgeneva.com

Project Managers: Leslie Johnson, Courtney Nobilio,
Michelle Goebel

Writers:
Martin Hintz (Hoppin' Into History, the Marcus Years)
Lisa M. Schmelz (Lake Geneva, Rock & Roll in the Country,
A Family Friendly Era)
Barbara Howell

Managing Editor: Barb Krause
Copyeditors: Anne Morrissy, Becky Peck
Design and Production: Kayla Collins

Published by:
Nei-Turner Media Group, Inc.
93 W. Geneva St., P.O. Box 1080
Williams Bay, WI 53191
262-245-1000
www.ntmediagroup.com

Printed in the U.S.A.

IN THE 1960S, LAKE GENEVA HAD BEEN THE PRIVATE PLAYGROUND of select Chicago millionaires for almost a century, a "Newport of the West" for a certain subset of the city to the south. But the town of Lake Geneva was otherwise provincial and insulated from the wider world, a summer haven hamlet of small roadside motels, mom-and-pop diners and a downtown that catered to local residents with necessities like pharmacies, hardware stores and groceries.

But in 1968, Playboy mogul Hugh Hefner put Lake Geneva on the international travel map when he opened one of the first of his highly-anticipated Playboy Club resorts on 1,300 acres just east of the city limits. Suddenly the once-insulated town welcomed entertainment superstars like Sonny and Cher, Joan Rivers, Bob Hope, Jerry Lewis and Liza Minnelli to the Playboy Club-Hotel's Penthouse Theater. The golf courses were considered some of the best resort courses in the country, one of them designed by famed golfer Jack Nicklaus himself. Almost overnight, Lake Geneva went from a staid, old-money getaway to the hottest travel destination in the Midwest.

Now under the stewardship of the Marcus Corporation, the AAA Four Diamond Grand Geneva Resort & Spa (formerly the Playboy Club-Hotel) consistently maintains its place on national "Best Of" lists, keeping Lake Geneva a top tourist travel destination for a whole new generation of travelers.

What began under the Playboy name in 1968 and continues today as Grand Geneva Resort & Spa has ushered in a new focus and identity for Lake Geneva. In this book, we examine the history of this pivotal resort property, beginning as the tale of an iconic tail (and the ears that went with it) and eventually evolving into a grand vacation destination.

Table of Contents

Lake Geneva:

EARLY YEARS AND NATIVE SOIL

YOU'VE LEFT THE CITY BEHIND. The entrance to Grand Geneva Resort & Spa is just ahead, a welcome landmark promising a much-deserved retreat from daily distractions. Pass through the Prairie-style gateway and begin the winding drive along Grand Geneva Way to the main lodge. Absorb the scenic rolling hills and lush, picturesque countryside, much like farmers and their families did decades ago, when they stood on these hills and fulfilled their American dreams of owning land.

Once you're here, there's no need to go anywhere else. Enjoy a few rounds of golf on nationally-recognized courses The Brute and The Highlands, a day spent at the WELL Spa + Salon, cocktails fireside at Embers Terrace: the possibilities are endless. It's an authentic Midwestern resort destination, just a short drive from the city and its urban anxiety. So much to do, or not do, all nestled within 1,300 acres in Lake Geneva.

The land that comprises the resort has a remarkable history. From immigrant farmers to Hugh Hefner and his bunnies, to a decline of the property followed by a phenomenal rejuvenation, the story of this property is one of extraordinary vision through decades of reincarnations.

Humble Beginnings

Records of Lake Geneva settlement date back to 1831, when U.S. Indian Agent John Kinzie and his party met with Chief Big Foot on the western shores of Geneva Lake. In 1834, government surveyor John Brink mapped the region and named the lake in honor of his hometown, Geneva, New York. Big Foot and his people were forced to leave two years later, and the village of Geneva was incorporated in 1844.

But the two events that bore the greatest influence on Lake Geneva's popularity were the re-introduction of passenger rail service and the Great Chicago Fire, both of which took place in 1871. From that moment on, well-to-do Chicago families

TOP: At one time or another, the Wrigleys have owned five estates along Geneva Lake. "Lakewood" was completed in 2014. © Holly Leitner BELOW: Originally owned by hotel tycoon Tracy Drake of the Drake Hotel, Aloha Lodge underwent expansions on either side of the original structure. Even with all its new modern touches, the Drake's china is still a part of this estate. © Clint Farlinger

flocked to the shores of Geneva Lake, earning it the nickname "The Newport of the West," for its similarities to Newport, Rhode Island's famed stretch of summer mansions. Situated among lush rolling hills, and anchored by a spring-fed lake, Lake Geneva had all the right ingredients to become a summer haven to captains of industry.

Chicago's Playground

Following the Chicago Fire, Lake Geneva provided a true refuge for traumatized families, who moved here while the Windy City rebuilt. Subsequently, many of Chicago's wealthiest and most important citizens made Lake Geneva their official second home. In the aftermath of the fire, they began to buy lakefront property and build expansive estates along the shores. Some of those estates still stand today, a testament to a different era.

Train service made it easy for Chicagoans to commute. By the turn of the century, well-known Chicago names such as Selfridge, Wacker and Drake all had homes here.

In 1906, Norman Wait Harris, founder of Harris Trust and Savings Bank, built one of the largest homes on the lake, now owned by Richard Driehaus. And in 1911, William Wrigley, Jr., founder of the Wm. Wrigley Jr. Company, purchased the first lakefront property of what would become hundreds of acres of family land ownership on Geneva Lake's north shore. More than a century later, the Wrigleys still own several lakefront estates here.

The Quiet Pastures

Just east of Lake Geneva, farmland was also sought after. The ownership lineage of the farmland that Grand Geneva sits on today can be traced through handwritten deeds at the county records office. Old Walworth County plat maps, painstakingly rendered by expert surveyors who recorded the past with pens and slide rules, offer the surnames of some of the landowners from the early 1900s, including Peller and Marubio.

Dominick Marubio, a European immigrant, bought 480 acres of land in the Town of Lyons. His grandson, Leo Marubio, recalls, "Grandpa bought the farm from Mr. McCormick and Grandpa said Mr. McCormick bought it from the Indians, but I don't know how true that is."

Many of the grand estates built in Lake Geneva by wealthy Chicagoans more than a century ago still stand today. Wadsworth Hall, now known as Glanworth Gardens and owned by Richard Driehaus, was built by Norman W. Harris in 1906. © Clint Farlinger

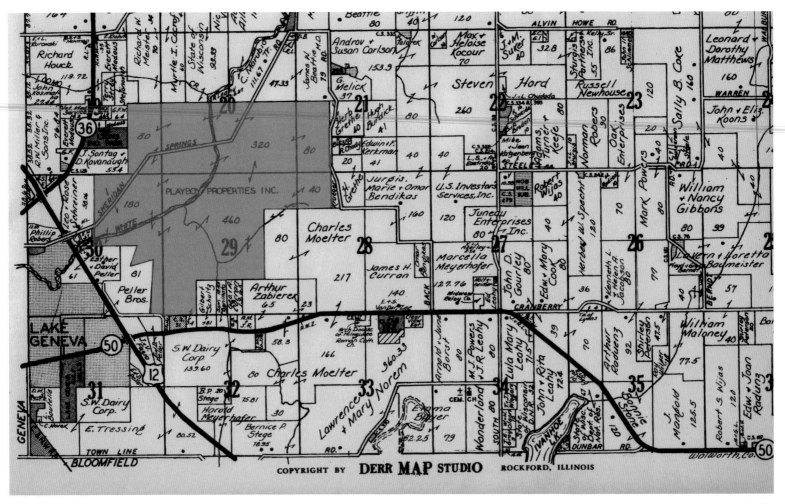

This plat map shows the acquired Playboy property (shaded, above). Playboy purchased the northern part of their property from the Marubio family. The Peller family sold 100 acres on the southwest side to Playboy for around $40,000.

"He [my grandfather] emigrated here as a child with his father," Marubio recalls, "and they read about the Chicago Fire in 1871 and felt that was a good place to get work. He started his teaming business in 1885."

By the time Leo Marubio began visiting the farm as a child in the 1940s and 1950s, the Town of Lyons "had one gas station, one general store, and a hitching post where you could tie up your horse," he remembers.

Horseback riding was one of Leo's favorite things to do here when he visited from Chicago. Specifically, he loved tackling Indian Knob, a natural rise in the land, which later became Playboy's ski hill. To Marubio, it was the closest a boy from Chicago could get to living a cowboy's dream.

Carl and Dave Peller, brothers who owned a butcher shop in Chicago, first acquired land here during the Great Depression. Ultimately, they would own 240 acres, part of which now comprises Grand Geneva. Like Dominick Marubio, they considered land as key to securing the American dream.

Carl Peller died in 1960, six years before Playboy came calling. Peller's family sold 100 of their 240 acres to Playboy for around $40,000. The price they had spent over the years for all 240 acres was just $42,000, Ed Peller recalls.

"It was wetlands," he says simply. "You wouldn't be able to touch it now. We used to get our tractor stuck in there all the time. . . . You couldn't plant anything. In fact, cows would get stuck. It was not a fit place for man or beast."

Grand Geneva's 1,300 acres of rolling countryside are a peaceful

However, Playboy was up for the challenge as they prepared to build their next club. They would tame and fill the land so that after the backhoes left, even a bunny in high heels could walk through it and not get stuck.

Meanwhile in Lake Geneva

Lake Geneva during that time period was a quaint place to raise a family, a small town that was on its way to growing a decent tourist economy. Conservative and rural, it seemed adept at doing the small town side-step when it came to major issues of the day. Even during the mid- and late-1960s, as the Civil Rights movement gained steam and opposition to the Vietnam War escalated, life in the Lake Geneva area was mostly peaceful and tranquil.

"It was very straight-laced . . . the town was very quiet in the winter, and busy in the summer. It was great growing up here. Everybody was friendly and nice, and things really didn't change that much," one local resident recalls.

Straight-laced or not, she does not recall Lake Geneva reacting with any sort of fuss over Playboy opening a club on the outskirts of town.

George Hennerley also grew up in Walworth County and served for many years as director of the Geneva Lake Area Chamber of Commerce. "It was described to me as the event that took Lake Geneva from being a Midwest-known destination to a nationally-known destination," he says today. "I don't think Lake Geneva would be what it is today had Playboy not showed up. It's similar, on a smaller scale, to the impact of Disney showing up in Orlando. Would Orlando have grown as much as it did without Disney buying a bunch of swamp land? Maybe I shouldn't say swamp land, but it changed things. It was a catalyst. That's what Playboy was for Lake Geneva, a catalyst."

"They brought in nationally-known entertainment," he says with a rapid-fire delivery. "They had a culinary school second to none. They had 350 [hotel] rooms out in the country, on a beautiful property. It's a nationally-known brand, with an image. People thought, 'This must be a cool place if Playboy is showing up.' That's hard to do on your own."

Leo Marubio (center) and his family owned 480 acres, where they enjoyed horseback riding and exploring the great outdoors. Tenant farmers managed the land. The barn (above) was located on the northern portion of land that is now Grand Geneva. Photos courtesy of Leo Marubio.

Horseback riding is still a popular activity at Grand Geneva. Dan Patch Stables offers guided trail rides, hay rides, and sleigh rides around the picturesque grounds.

Lake Geneva Before Playboy

Lake Geneva's story did not start with Playboy, of course, though the arrival of the bunnies certainly helped to spur the area's increase in tourism. Rather, the rolling glacial terrain of the area and sparkling, spring-fed waters of Geneva Lake speak of an era thousands of years earlier, when the glaciers that moved through the area created the lush landscape that we enjoy today.

The largest mansion on the lake, Stone Manor, was built in 1899 for Otto Young and his family. © Clint Farlinger

Shore Path

The mansions built around the lake represent every style of architecture, including Italian Renaissance, Georgian Revival and Queen Anne styles. Along the approximately twenty-one mile shore path — which is completely open to the public — lie several magnificently preserved, turn-of-the-century estates. Stroll the path and it's easy to understand how the construction and maintenance of these mansions provided an economic boost to the town. Walking the entire path takes eight to ten hours, but it provides an up-close view of the history of Lake Geneva.

Stone Manor

The mansion now known as Stone Manor was the largest single-family home on the lake when it was built by Otto Young in 1899. Young made his money in shrewd real estate investments and jewelry imports, and would become the third richest man in Chicago, with only Marshall Field and Levi Leiter in front of him. Henry Lord Gay designed the ornate, Beaux Arts-style mansion, originally called Younglands. When built, each of the structure's upper floors and three underground levels was 12,400 square feet. Over the years, it has been a restaurant, a Christmas tree museum, and also came close to being an Air Force Academy. It is now luxury condominiums, with a rooftop pool and underground parking garage.

The Geneva Lake shore path is open to the public and offers many unique points of interest along the way. © Holly Leitner

Lake Geneva was also the home of Sidney Smith, creator of the Andy Gump comic strip. (A statue of Andy Gump stands in a park in downtown Lake Geneva.) More recently, William Bell and Lee Phillip Bell, the creators and producers of the popular soap opera "The Young and The Restless," had a home here — Casa del Sueño — and found inspiration for the naming of their soap's fictional town nearby, choosing to borrow the name Genoa City (located ten miles south of Lake Geneva).

Riviera Ballroom

In downtown Lake Geneva, the Riviera Ballroom remains a major landmark on the lakeshore. It was built at the height of the Great Depression in 1932 on a man-made peninsula of 280 pilings driven directly into the bedrock. During the Swing Era of the 1930s and 1940s, 'The Riv,' as it's known locally, played host to Big Band names like Wayne King, the Dorseys, Artie Shaw, and Louis Armstrong.

In fact, Armstrong is credited with racially integrating The Riviera. In the 1960s, a group of African-Americans was denied entrance to Armstrong's show. They tried to take their case straight to the famed trumpeter on his tour bus parked nearby, but were intercepted by his manager. When word reached Armstrong, it is reported he informed Riviera management that he would not perform unless everyone — regardless of skin color — was admitted.

Today, the Riviera houses several shops in the lower level, and the upper level serves as a civic center and ballroom.

Yerkes Observatory

Yerkes Observatory, operated by the University of Chicago since 1897, towers over the treetops in nearby Williams Bay. It has been the site of many important discoveries over the years, including the detection of carbon dioxide in the atmosphere around Mars and the finding of Uranus' fifth moon and Neptune's second moon, among others. Yerkes Observatory was one of two places Albert Einstein asked to see on his 1921 tour of America (the other being Niagara Falls).

Yerkes still houses the world's largest refracting telescope in its huge dome. The observatory is open for public tours on Saturdays and often hosts seminars and lectures by its scientists.

Today, Lake Geneva has a year-round population of just over 7,600. Tourism continues to be a driving force in the county's economy, exceeding over $409 million annually.

The Riviera Ballroom was added to the National Register of Historic Places in 1986. © Kayla Collins

Operated by the University of Chicago since 1897, Yerkes Observatory was one of two places Albert Einstein asked to see on his 1921 tour of America, the other being Niagara Falls. Yerkes remains an active observatory, and its refracting telescope is still the world's largest. © Clint Farlinger

Hoppin' Into History

HUGH HEFNER AND HIS PLAYBOY BUNNIES COME TO TOWN

WHEN THE PLAYBOY CLUB-HOTEL WAS COMPLETED in 1968, it was like nothing the Lake Geneva area had yet seen. The grounds were picturesque. The architecture was ahead of its time. The food was fantastic and service over-the-top. The music and entertainment were nationally recognized. The bunnies were gorgeous. Taken together, the Playboy Club-Hotel represented the epitome of the era's decadence and sophistication, a resort where those in the know could ski, horseback ride, dine, and be up-close and almost personal to the world's top performers.

Southeastern Wisconsin, or at least the picturesque community of Lake Geneva, would never be the same after Hugh Hefner and his entourage arrived in the 1960s. Less than two hours' drive from either Milwaukee or Chicago, Lake Geneva provided a scenic location for developing a major vacation destination, drawing visitors from around the world.

In 1953, a man named Hugh Hefner launched a small business that would eventually rock the world. Playboy Enterprises Inc. was created as the HMH Publishing Co. Inc. for the purpose of publishing the eyebrow-raising *Playboy* magazine.

After launching the magazine, Hefner proved he was a savvy businessman as *Playboy* magazine circulation soon soared past one million. Advertising revenues quickly zoomed to $2.3 million. To the envy of frat boys from coast-to-coast, Hefner was a "Man of Action," supposedly a sexual colossus able to date seven women at once and brag of snuggling with more than 1,000 others. However, Hefner always said he was faithful during his marriage to wife Mildred, with whom he had a daughter, Christie, and a son, David. Christie went on to be chief executive officer of Playboy Enterprises. Hugh and Mildred Hefner divorced in 1959 after a decade of marriage.

Hugh Hefner in 1955. © Getty Images

Buoyed by his publishing success, Hefner decided to branch out, with the help of Victor Lownes. Lownes observed the success of Burton Brown's chain of Gaslight Clubs, launched in 1953. The bistros featured attractive young women dressed in formfitting one-piece velvet outfits as servers. From this model, Lownes spotted a golden opportunity to expand the Playboy image. Hefner and Lownes were aided in this endeavor by Arnold "Arnie" Morton, a well-known restaurateur who would later open Morton's of Chicago.

Playboy Enters the Resort Business

The new Playboy Club concept was straightforward. It would be a destination where a business executive could eat, drink, entertain, and be served by, perhaps, a Playboy bunny named Merry. The latter would be a gorgeous young thing, crowned with rabbit ears and skimpily clothed in nothing more than a formfitting, one-piece corset. The crowning touch was a cotton tail fixed to the bunny's derriere.

The first Playboy Club opened on February 29, 1960, at 116 East Walton Street in downtown Chicago. The concept proved to be a hit with the clubbing public; business boomed. During the last three months of 1961, more than 132,000 people packed into the Chicago bunny playground, making it the world's most bustling nightclub. Membership was only $25 a year for the privilege of pocketing one of the highly valued, rabbit-headed metal medallions. Membership was a status symbol, although barely twenty-one percent of all key holders ever visited the club.

In late November, 1964, Arnie Morton held a press conference in New York to describe properties that Playboy International was considering developing in London and Paris. The London property would include a casino. But what caught the attention of Wisconsinites was the news that Playboy was considering a plush multi-million-dollar resort hotel in the Lake Geneva area. The announcement lacked details but quickly set off a flurry of speculation in the area. News reports quoted Morton as saying the project would include a two hundred-room hotel in the Playboy motif, with swimming pools, ski areas, and an eighteen-hole golf course, at rates of $5 to $100 a day.

Beginning in 1965, Hefner spent more than $55 million to develop his string of resort hotels. His Ochos Rios Club, Hotel & Resort in Jamaica opened on January 4, 1965, and the London Casino & Club debuted on July 1, 1966. Additionally during this time, Hefner's corporate reach extended from building Playboy apartment complexes to negotiating a deal with Columbia Pictures to make mainline movies. He produced television shows, cut records, and published sheet music. From 1965 to 1970, sales at Playboy Enterprises Inc. leapt skyward, from $48 million to a mind-boggling $127 million.

Key Players

© Getty Images

Victor Lownes

After helping Hugh Hefner establish his Playboy empire in the United States, Chicago pitchman Victor Lownes left in 1963 to head Playboy Europe and the UK Playboy Clubs. He held this position from the mid-1960s until his firing in the early 1980s. At one time, Lownes was Britain's highest-paid executive, with a salary of $113,800. In addition, he was Playboy Enterprises' second-largest shareholder.

In 1981, Lownes became senior vice president responsible for Hefner's worldwide network of casinos, the moneymaking part of the Playboy operation. He led the effort to open up Atlantic City, New Jersey, to gambling.

However, while living in Britain, Lownes was accused of financial wrongdoing by the country's gaming authorities. The charges were never proven, but before he could appear in court, Lownes was fired, allegedly in an attempt to save the New Jersey deal. The British gaming license was revoked, which had long-reaching financial effects on the corporation, effects that eventually had a serious impact on the Lake Geneva Playboy Club-Hotel. Adding insult to injury, Playboy's temporary gaming license in Atlantic City was not renewed, either.

Arnie Morton

In addition to his work with Hefner in developing the Playboy Clubs, Arnold "Arnie" Morton founded Morton's Restaurant Group which included the well-known Morton's Steakhouse, which now has over seventy locations.

Morton grew up on Chicago's south side and from an early age bussed tables and worked in the kitchen of his father's restaurant. He opened his first restaurant, the Walton Walk, between Rush Street and Michigan Avenue in the 1950s. Soon after he met Hefner and Lownes and opened the first Playboy Club.

One of Morton's innovative ideas at Playboy inspired a merchandising division, which started marketing and selling souvenir items featuring the Playboy logo.

Morton left Playboy in the early 1970s and launched several clubs including Arnie's, followed by Zorine's, a tribute to his wife, and finally, Morton's Steakhouse. He sold the Morton's franchise of more than sixty locations in 1987.

Morton passed away in 2005. His children and grandchildren are continuing the family tradition with successful restaurants of their own.

© Playboy Enterprises, Inc.

Dick Rosenzweig

Dick Rosenzweig has been Hugh Hefner's right hand man for the last 55 years, and served as the executive vice president of Playboy Enterprises, Inc., from 1988 to 2011. Today, the Appleton, Wisconsin native works as a consultant to Hefner and his iconic brand.

Dick recalls the thinking behind Playboy's initial search for one of its first resort properties. "When we looked at the demographics and a map," he explains from his office in California, "and we drew a circle around [Lake Geneva] and we noted that Lake Geneva is between Chicago and Milwaukee, with millions of people, it's only logical . . . it was a kind of test on 'Should we be in the hotel business?'"

Starting in 1968 and for the next 13 years, Playboy would introduce tourists from around the world to Walworth County, and specifically Lake Geneva, pumping millions into the local economy.

"To my recollection," says Rosenzweig, "there was no upscale competition for that kind of facility. It was a beautiful facility in every way. Not merely the hotel, and the attending spaces, but the grounds really took one away from a different life if one wanted to get away. It was a perfect holiday destination."

Lake Geneva Plans Become Reality

As Playboy Enterprises Inc. quietly began purchasing acreage in the area, the word got out that Indian Knob was the appointed site. In 1966, Playboy had assembled some 1,300 acres purchased under the name of Club Land Development Corporation. Their plans included a hotel in the heart of a complex that would eventually include two championship golf courses, horse stables, swimming pools, and a ski hill. Later, in looking over the Playboy Club-Hotel's finished version, Morton said, "We've created a total environment here. You have the feeling that even if you're from Chicago or Milwaukee or right down the road, you're very, very far from home the moment you drive through the gates." The Lake Geneva resort was intended to be the company's flagship resort complex, costing a total of $18 million. (The hotel alone cost $8 million.) The venue became the twentieth of more than forty properties in Hugh Hefner's ever-expanding empire.

Hefner contracted with architects Robert L. Taege of Barrington, Illinois, and Chicagoan Paul Magierek on the design and construction of the new site. Both men were highly respected for their innovative designs and ability to turn in a project in- or under-budget. Taege was involved in the development of the original Playboy Club in Chicago in 1958 and was the architect of the Detroit, Kansas City, and Cincinnati clubs.

Hefner also hired interior designer Richard Himmel to work on the project. Himmel's outgoing personality and artistic lifestyle were attractive to Hefner. Himmel was creatively multifaceted, as were most of Hefner's top collaborators.

A Glamorous Groundbreaking

The official groundbreaking of the Lake Geneva Playboy Club-Hotel took place on Friday, August 26, 1966, with typical Hefner flourish. Roaring up from Chicago, Hefner arrived via a Sikorsky S58 helicopter; its powerful propellers setting the grass waving and dust flying. In addition to two crew members, Hefner was accompanied by six glamorous bunnies in shoulder-revealing evening gowns. Other femmes fatale imported from the Chicago Playboy Club had arrived earlier by motorcoach. With Hefner's dramatic entrance, it was obvious that the ceremony would be no ordinary hard-hat-and-shovel photo opportunity.

Grip-and-grinning politicians — including Lake Geneva's mayor, and a bevy of local movers and shakers — turned out to greet the Playboy contingent. The Lyons Volunteer Fire Department happily agreed to be on hand, when asked to stand by in case of emergency. Wearing a red hard hat with a Playboy logo, and accompanied by bunnies chanting "five, four, three, two, one," Hefner pushed a button to set off a dynamite charge blasting out a deep hole atop Indian Knob, where Leo Marubio had once ridden his horse. With this,

Hefner blasted a deep hole atop Indian Knob at the official ground-breaking ceremony on August 26, 1966. Courtesy of the *Lake Geneva Regional News*.

TOP: Seven interconnected buildings would overlook a manmade lake. BELOW: Architects Robert Taege (center) and Paul Magierek (left) review their work with a contractor on the roof of the main building. Photos courtesy of Don McElfresh.

a vast column of smoke and chunks of earth rose into the air as onlookers gasped and covered their ears.

The gala celebration continued. An array of Wisconsin cheeses were offered on silver trays and sirloin steaks were grilled under a big top tent. Overhead, planes circled, dropping a quartet of skydivers. The last jumper had a blazing torch affixed to his helmet and carried a Playboy flag.

Under a bright blue sky and fronted by numerous photographers, Hefner stepped up to the microphone and described his goals and plans for the resort, speaking to a rapt audience perched on bleacher seats erected for the event. To the ex-hilarated crowd, he indicated that the site was chosen because of its proximity to large population centers and "Lake Geneva's background as a known resort area." Hefner pointed out that the complex was expected to employ 250, with a payroll of upwards of $1.3 million a year. There was more applause when the suave Chicagoan said that the Lake Geneva complex would be the "first and foremost" of several resort concepts Playboy was planning around the country.

It took three years to plan and construct the 265,000-square-foot building. Above-ground construction started in the winter of 1966; the first concrete was poured while snow was still on the ground. Working within Taege and Magierek's archi-tectural concepts, interior designer Richard Himmel included many elements of European styling, but both he and Hefner were fans of the era's clean lines.

The architects had worked with landscapers to promote a timeless feeling, devising a long, winding drive called the Cottontail Trail that took motorists through the scenic countryside to the main lodge. A key card was presented to guests as they arrived at the guard gate. At night, wrought iron gas lanterns cast a flickering glow on the lanes winding between crabapple trees, maples, and Douglas firs, all designed to showcase the resort's four-season appeal.

Seven interconnected buildings made up the five-acre central complex overlooking the manmade Playboy Lake. The structures had a touch of Frank Lloyd Wright's Taliesin in their design, emulating the Prairie style architecture with which Wright is most often associated. Taege and Magierek emphasized strong, horizontal lines, with wide expanses of bronze-tinted solar glass that seemed to invite the world outside to come in. This was their signature: "visual effect of unity with the sur-roundings," striving for the feel of a Camelot in the country. Frank Lloyd Wright's style focused on his deep appreciation for nature, aligning his structures with the horizontal line of the land, blending it into its setting.

Grubbing and staking of the golf courses began in the fall of 1967 and the greens were expected to fill in nicely for the projected June opening the fol-lowing year. Six small lakes dotted the courses and were stocked with trout

CONTINUED ON PAGE 29

upper level floor plan

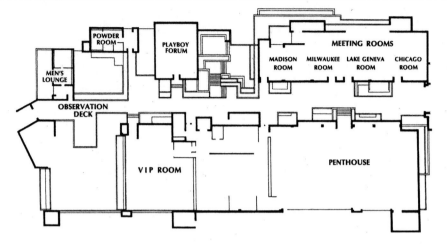

POWDER ROOM

PLAYBOY FORUM

MEETING ROOMS

MADISON ROOM   MILWAUKEE ROOM   LAKE GENEVA ROOM   CHICAGO ROOM

MEN'S LOUNGE

OBSERVATION DECK

VIP ROOM

PENTHOUSE

the ski chalet

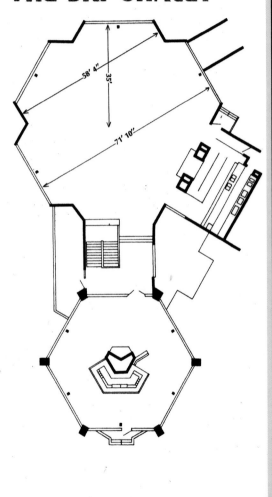

58' 4"

35'

71' 10"

main level floor plan

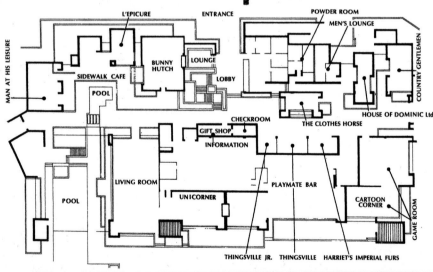

L'EPICURE   ENTRANCE

POWDER ROOM

MEN'S LOUNGE

MAN AT HIS LEISURE

SIDEWALK CAFE

BUNNY HUTCH

LOUNGE

LOBBY

POOL

COUNTRY GENTLEMEN

HOUSE OF DOMINIC Ltd.

THE CLOTHES HORSE

CHECKROOM

GIFT SHOP

INFORMATION

LIVING ROOM

POOL

UNICORNER

PLAYMATE BAR

CARTOON CORNER

GAME ROOM

THINGSVILLE JR.   THINGSVILLE   HARRIET'S IMPERIAL FURS

The Playboy Club-Hotel marketed its new facilities as an "inn for all seasons" and "the perfect playground for business."

The Lake Geneva Playboy Club-Hotel had its own airport, and seeing the resort from the air was exciting for guests, especially as the golf fairways and ponds came into view. On the south side of the runway was the ski hill, surrounded by a bar, restaurant, and pool. Along the north side of the runway and taxiway were the skeet and trap range, as well as the barn and stables. Many pilots flew in for lunch and departed soon after. Landing fees were $3 in the mid-1970s, bringing in around $18,000 a year. Fliers needing a car could rent from National, which had offices at the Club.
© Bill Frantz

Several manmade lakes were constructed on the property. One was designed in the shape of a heart, and another as an abstract bunny head. © Bill Frantz

CONTINUED FROM PAGE 24

and large-mouth bass. The water performed double duty as the courses' sprinkling system.

One of the 18-hole golf courses, the par-71, 6,900-yard Briar Patch, was a Scottish design by famous golfer Jack Nicklaus and course designer Pete Dye. The second course, the par-72 Brute, was created by Robert Bruce Harris, measuring 7,256 yards. The courses were built into the hilly terrain and scattered woods, a natural amphitheater for their eighteen holes. Harris' course was carved out of the countryside, while the Nicklaus-Dye project worked with the land's contours.

A New Era Begins

The grand opening of the Lake Geneva Playboy Club-Hotel took place on May 6, 1968, with even more fanfare than the ground-breaking.

On the glittering grand opening night, guests were received like royalty and women received sample bottles of Playboy signature perfumes. A jazz trio played and a disco dance room featured a bunny D.J. People were everywhere, filling the parking lots, gift shops, and overflowing the lobby. The Playboy logo was everywhere: on ash trays, glasses, drink stirrers, pens, and stationery.

World-class Accommodations

The Playboy Club-Hotel quickly became the crown jewel of Lake Geneva. The entry flowed into a plush lobby with its sunken lounge centered around a glass-backed gas fireplace and rimmed with tropical plants. Pebble-textured concrete aggregate walls and rough-hewn wooden beams rounded out the impression of masculinity. Guests arriving at night could see past the fireplace into the Bunny Hutch discothéque.

The Clothes Horse boutique peddled both beach bags and Dior originals. If one's wife or girlfriend dreamed of a jasmine mink bikini, a guest simply visited Harriet's Imperial Furs. The Playboy Gift Shop was the place for all things Playboy-logo.

ABOVE: Golf Pro Ken Judd poses on the course with Frankie Avalon. © Bill Frantz LEFT: The Briar Patch scorecard. The course was renovated in 1997 by Bob Cupp and renamed The Highlands.

Tales of a Bellman

Allen Anderson, a native son of Williams Bay, began work at the Playboy Club-Hotel in May of 1968, several weeks prior to its opening. He was working as a desk clerk at the nearby Abbey Resort where a number of the Playboy corporate management team stayed during the resort's construction. Subsequently, Anderson got to know them fairly well, so they invited him to join the staff at Playboy.

After six months as a desk clerk, Anderson observed how much money the bellmen were apparently making. He requested a transfer to the bell stand where in his first week he made more than $400 in cash. The bellman's earnings were made by sheer volume, since the hourly wage was only eighty-five cents an hour. But the average tip was $2 or $3, and a $5 tip, also known as a "fin," was great.

Arriving guests were met curbside by the doorman and were instructed in most cases to leave all their luggage in their vehicles. Visitors had to be escorted to their rooms as a matter of policy. This was to give them all information on dining and entertainment options and other resort amenities, as well as carrying their luggage. Once the guest was registered, they returned to their vehicles and followed bellmen in electric carts to the parking area closest to their room. The bellmen then unloaded their cars from the parking lot and used two-wheel carts to bring the luggage to the rooms.

Due to the architecture of the building, there were stair wells between each of the guest wings. This necessitated pulling the loaded luggage carts up one or more flights of stairs, or carrying all of the luggage without a cart. The bellmen had some amazing techniques for carrying more luggage and hanging bags than appeared possible. Putting on a bit of a show usually earned larger tips.

The barbershop and a hair salon ensured that patrons always looked their best. The Playmate Bar featured enlarged photos of the Playmates of the Month, framed in wood and back lit. Outside, hidden spotlights illuminated the trees.

There were 350 rooms, including celebrity and VIP suites that featured round beds, wet bars, color televisions, and fireplaces. The Hugh M. Hefner Penthouse was also available for rent, with room for 200 guests for cocktails and buffet in the fifty-by-forty-foot living room.

However, Hefner's own accommodations at the Lake Geneva Playboy Club-Hotel were modest by comparison. Suite 4318 consisted of a lounge and two adjoining bedrooms, shag carpeting, a fireplace, and the iconic round bed. The stereo and sound system were hidden behind a bookcase that could be activated

by a switch beside the bed. Albums were available out of sight, plucked from racks, just like a regular jukebox. For the most exclusive parties, insider gossip rumored, the Jacuzzi was sometimes filled with the contents of up to fifty bottles of Dom Perignon champagne.

Many guests started their beverage expedition in the Playmate Bar on the main level, which offered a panoramic daytime view of the grounds, lake, and golf course. While some dined here, devouring the homemade bread and fresh cocktail shrimp, others downed their martinis and strolled over to the buffet in the Living Room. For this restaurant, Himmel collaborated with artist LeRoy Neiman to create a contemporary impression of

ABOVE: Suites were designed by Richard Himmel. BELOW: The plush lobby featured a sunken lounge centered around a fireplace.

The Penthouse could accommodate up to 400 guests. This upper level room is now the Grand Geneva's Evergreen Ballroom. © Bill Frantz

The Bandleader

Italian-American jazz pianist and entertainment manager Sam Distefano had an extended stint with Playboy International, including a promotion to musical director at the Playboy Club in Miami from 1962 to 1969. He went on to become the orchestra leader, conductor, and entertainment director at the Lake Geneva club from 1969 to 1978, where he led his own swinging thirty-two-piece orchestra, accompanying on piano. Distefano conducted for artists such as Peggy Lee, Mel Tormé, Anthony Newley, Tony Bennett, the Smothers Brothers, Liza Minnelli, and Ann-Margret, among many others. When not performing, he sat at Table Number One where he had the best view of the stage, drinking only Coca-Cola. Showroom manager Carlo Cicirello always made it a point to deliver the soda in an iced champagne bucket, with a white napkin draped over his arm. (Hefner was also a Coke guy, but augmented his bubbly beverage with value-added Jack Daniels.)

Noted for his well-tailored three-piece suits, the always-dapper Distefano eventually became vice president of entertainment for Playboy's entire international chain of clubs and hotels worldwide. He also served as executive producer of the Playboy Fantasy production show and revue at the Playboy Hotel and Casino in Atlantic City from 1981 to 1983. He was retained as a consultant for Playboy through the end of 1984. After that, Distefano headed to Las Vegas where he became vice president of entertainment and special events at the Riviera Hotel and Casino. He retired from the Riviera in 1993 and formed his own entertainment management and consulting firm with his drummer son, Michael, who grew up at the Lake Geneva Playboy Club-Hotel while his dad worked there.

what they thought a medieval hunting lodge might look like.

On the upper level, the VIP Room earned a reputation as one of the country's best restaurants. Muted dinner conversation was accompanied by the clink of quality crystal and the scrape of sword-sized knives carving into juicy, tender prime rib. Ten nearby meeting rooms with names like Milwaukee, Madison, Lake Geneva, and Chicago could accommodate forty to 480 people; the Penthouse alone seated 400 guests.

Stars Stream into Lake Geneva

Lownes and Hefner particularly appreciated the talents of noted Windy City band leader Sam Distefano, who performed with his jazz trio at the Playboy Club in Chicago. This launched what would turn into Distefano's twenty-five year career with Playboy, including a stint as entertainment director at the Lake Geneva resort. Because he was a musician himself and knew many of Playboy's top-rate lineup of entertainers, Distefano was a huge asset for Playboy. Among his many performer friends gracing Lake Geneva's stages from the Playboy circuit were Bob Hope, Sonny & Cher, Tony Bennett, Liza Minnelli, Diahann Carroll, Peggy Lee, The Smothers Brothers, Frankie Avalon, The Monkees, Milton Berle, George Carlin, Mel Tormé, Jerry Lewis, Ann-Margret, Doc Severinsen, Joan Rivers, Bobby Rydell, Frank Sinatra, Sammy Davis, Jr., Phyllis Diller, and Louie Nye.

Most of the female performers — Cher, Phyllis Diller, Peggy Lee, and Lainie Kazan, among others — cozied up their dressing spaces with family photos and other personal items. The male artists were often more interested in what "attractions" were already on the property. A number of the stars had extensive "riders" on their contracts, demanding

Sports celebrities also frequented the resort, including freestyle skier Wayne Wong. © Bill Frantz

A day-long Bluegrass Jamboree was held at the ski hill in July 1977.
© Bill Frantz

Playboy constructed a year-round, heated swimming pool at the ski hill, popular with guests. It closed in the mid-1970s after it fell into disrepair. Courtesy of Playboy.

specific comforts. Jerry Lewis' ten-page add-on even indicated the specific wattage of the light bulbs he preferred. As a rule, Distefano indulged them.

Security at the Playboy Club-Hotel was taken very seriously and there was a zero-tolerance policy when it came to protecting the bunnies and visiting celebrities, both on and off the property. No drunken or disorderly conduct was tolerated. "Touch a tail and you're outta here" was the mantra. In addition, Showroom Manager Carlo Cicirello had a direct line to the Walworth County Sheriff's Department. The deputies always jumped at the chance to respond to a call from the Club.

For certain celebs like Tony Bennett, Liza Minnelli, and Peggy Lee, Hefner relinquished his own room, Suite 4318, down the hall from the showroom. But there were some lavish suites in the east wing as well, where artists such as Freddie Prinze and Frankie Avalon stayed.

Most shows were well received and often covered on television. Tony Bennett was noted for his "socko night club finish" each time he performed in Lake Geneva. For his July 1970 appearance, the dark-suited, white-shirted, narrow-tie-wearing Bennett crooned through five straight sellouts in the Penthouse, at $7.50 per head cover charge.

Singer Lainie Kazan loved to arrive 10 to 15 minutes late to keep the audience anxious and eager for her glamorous entrance. The orchestra simply played an overture in the meantime until she appeared onstage. This habit really got under Cicirello's skin. One night, he told her the showtime had been changed to 7:30 instead of 8 p.m. Subsequently, she arrived 15 minutes early. When she discovered the curtain wasn't up yet and the orchestra hadn't struck the first note, the singer hurled insults at Cicirello while he stood there and grinned.

So Much To Do

Whether they arrived by motorcoach, auto, or plane, guests had plenty of diversions at the rollicking Playboy Club-Hotel. In the early days, greens fees for golf were only $6 for residents and $9 for non-residents. Men's or

The Playboy Club-Hotel's many on-site activities included a mini-golf course (above) and a trap and skeet range (below). © Bill Frantz

The ski lodge was designed in the shape of two intersecting snowflakes by Alexander McIlvaine, the architect who created the Squaw Valley complex for the 1960 Winter Olympics in California. © Bill Frantz

women's five-speed Schwinn bicycles rented for $2 an hour, and twenty rounds and a gun were available at the range for $5.50. Visitors could get a sightseeing plane tour for $5 per person, and a chairlift ride to the top of Playboy's ski hill was $1 off-season for the scenic overlook. For $7.50, wine and a picnic basket would be provided. Carriage rides around the property were also offered.

The Lake Geneva Fitness and Racquet Centre was only about 150 yards from the main building. Often entertainers would visit the courts to limber up. In 1980, tennis instructor George Hansen umpired a doubles match between the U.S. Clay Court champion Frankie Parker, grand slammer Don Budge (who wielded a deadly swing with his vintage Prince Woodie racquet), actor Desi Arnaz, Jr., and singer Dino Martin, Dean Martin's son who was a noted tennis competitor.

The Playboy Ski Area thrived under the direction of Gerald Shanley, recruited from Pennsylvania's Camelback Mountain Ski Resort. The chalet was designed by Alexander McIlvaine, while Shanley supervised the construction and assisted in the installation of two Hall chairlifts; one on the main slope and one on the bunny slope.

The ski slopes were originally intended only for the private use of Playboy Club members. But in 1971, with the promotion of group lessons to school and business groups, the slopes were opened to the skiing public.

At that time, The Ray T. Stemper Ski School was contracted to operate the ski school under the direction of Jim Engel. Jim came to the Playboy Club-Hotel after serving as the assistant ski school director at nearby Alpine Valley Ski Area in East Troy. His wife, Kim (along with Ray Stemper's

Bunnies Crea, Dona and Lee pose on the ski hill.
© Bill Frantz

CONTINUED ON PAGE 40

Gail Hintz Frantz began at the Lake Geneva Playboy Club-Hotel as a bunny at age 18, starting just two weeks after the grand opening. She later took over as "Bunny Mother," managing 125 bunnies and also served as Corporate Trainer for Playboy Hotels. Photos courtesy of Gail Hintz Frantz.

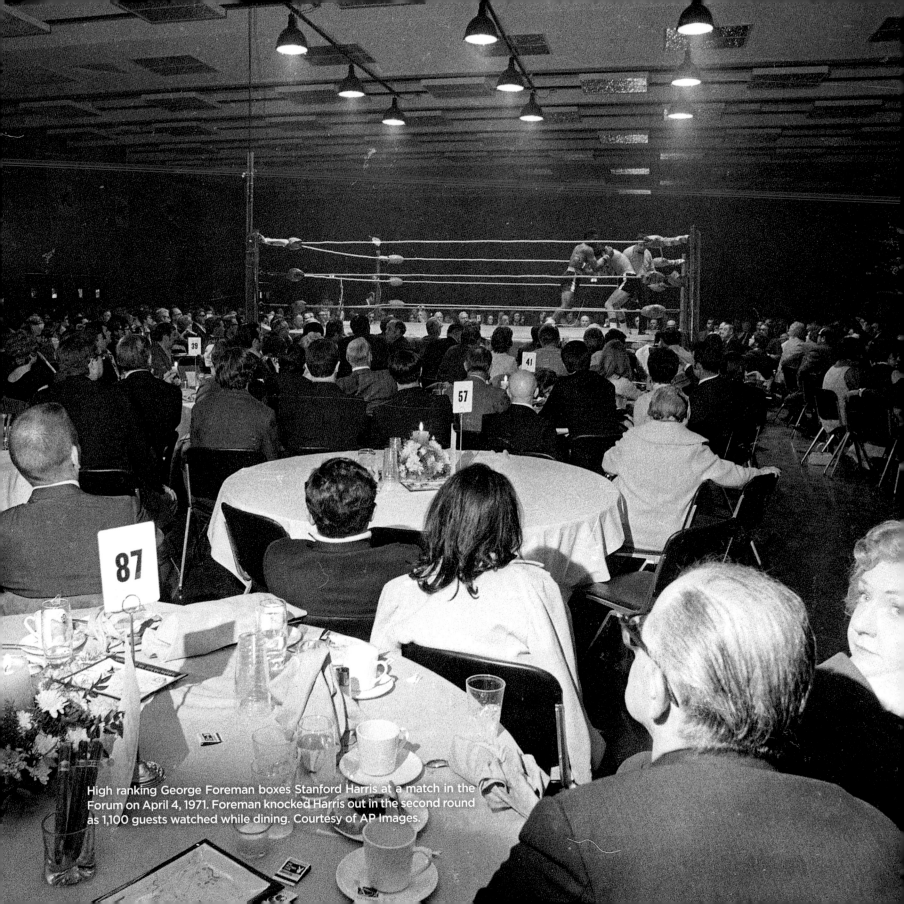

High ranking George Foreman boxes Stanford Harris at a match in the Forum on April 4, 1971. Foreman knocked Harris out in the second round as 1,100 guests watched while dining. Courtesy of AP Images.

Celebrity Sightings

Bill Pullen was watching television several years ago when he came across an interview with the late comedian George Carlin. Carlin was telling the interviewer the story of the time he had been fired after a performance at the Playboy Club-Hotel. It was a day Pullen remembered well; he had done the firing. "[Carlin] of course was known as a kind of brash entertainer, and this was during the height of the Vietnam era," he said. "He was doing some stuff on Vietnam and our entertainment director had said to him, 'We're not Manhattan, we're in the cornfields of Wisconsin — you have to ease up on the politics a little bit.' He didn't take the advice.

"On Saturday night, the place was packed, the curtain had just gone up, when I was called back because of a disturbance. The audience was just streaming out of the theater. I worked my way through the crowd like a fish swimming upstream. I'm not going to tell you exactly what [Carlin] told the audience, but he was very vulgar, and the audience didn't like it. He walked off the stage a few minutes into the show."

Pullen served as the Managing Director of the Playboy Club-Hotel from 1970 to 1972. While there, he had his share of celebrity encounters, most of which ended on a much better note than his encounter with Carlin. "We had Sonny & Cher [performing with us] for nine days at the peak of their career. It was a time when they had just taped a six-week series on CBS and they got fantastic reviews and we had them between the second and third week of those shows being aired by CBS. Every show they did for us was sold out, but Sonny was solicited by some of the bunnies who wanted to see the show. Sonny asked if we could add a second show on Sunday evening just for the employees. So we did — we had employees and their spouses. And Sonny & Cher actually put on a better show for the employees."

Pullen came to the Playboy Club-Hotel after

Bill Pullen poses with entertainer Diahann Carroll.

working as a manager with Restaurant Associates in New York City, one of the top restaurant groups in the world at the time. He had taken a job in Scottsdale, Arizona when he was recruited to become the Managing Director at the Lake Geneva Playboy Club-Hotel by Ken Abrams, who had been the vice president of human resources at Restaurant Associates but now worked for Playboy.

It was a time when the corporation was working hard to promote its expanding resort business, and the Lake Geneva location served as the perfect spot to host promotional exhibitions. For one such stunt, Pullen says, "Brunswick came and built two bowling alleys in the conference center from scratch. ABC used it to film a 'Best of Bowling' series, where celebrities bowled against pros. We also did a boxing exhibition featuring George Foreman and Ernie Terrell doing three-round exhibitions. For that, we built a boxing ring in the middle of the conference center. That was also televised."

The state-of-the-art golf course drew celebrities from the world of sports, including [former Green Bay Packers' quarterback] Bart Starr and [golf legends] Arnold Palmer and Jack Nicklaus. (In fact, Nicklaus had helped design one of the golf courses on the property.) During one golf pro-am tournament, GM Division President Martin Caserio was playing the back nine when a call came into the pro shop for him from President Richard M. Nixon. "I sent a bunny out in a golf cart to get him, but the bunny came back without him. Apparently he'd said, 'Just tell him I'll call him back when I'm through.'"

Pullen eventually left the Playboy Club-Hotel to take over the management of the Carefree Resort in Scottsdale, Arizona. "Having endured two winters in Wisconsin, [Arizona] became very desirable. But [my family and I] love Wisconsin. We made some good friends and met some good employees there."

Many Lake Geneva Playboy Club-Hotel bunnies have fond memories of meeting the celebrities who entertained here, including Bob Hope. © Bill Frantz

CONTINUED FROM PAGE 37

wife, Diane), also worked at Playboy as a group coordinator, booking ski groups. Kim Engel trained new ski instructors during "dry land" ski training season, preparing them to teach students once snowmaking began in December.

In 1976, Shanley and Engel suggested that more dirt be brought in, creating better intermediate terrain and a much larger beginner teaching area; two rope tows were installed in the Playboy Teaching Corral. In 1978, Playboy added new expert terrain and called it "Hotdog Mountain," installing another chairlift that summer.

Close Quarters: The Bunny Dorm

As for the bunnies, many of them lived in a separate dorm on the resort grounds. A chain-link fence topped with barbed wire surrounded the building, with a security lock on the gate. No men were allowed in the Bunny Dorm. The living arrangements were similar to college dormitories, where some of the women had one or two roommates. There was a galley kitchen that was rarely used. Most rooms had small refrigerators. The rooms shared a communal bathroom, with several women forced to crowd around sinks and compete for use of the shower stalls. The hotel housekeeping staff cleaned the facility, much to the relief of the hardworking bunny crew. A "Dorm Bunny" was in charge of residents, keeping a careful watch over her charges. Rent was $90 a month and included use of a washer and dryer, one that was shared between at least sixty women.

The dorm was a place to sleep and shower, with a centrally located television room. However, the set was rarely turned on because naptime and laundry were usually foremost demands between shifts. The bunnies could eat for half-price at the resort or dine free in the cafeteria, but most preferred to eat out as a break from their work routine.

Great Expectations

Competition to become a bunny was tough. Women were selected from auditions and underwent a strict two-week training regime that consisted of forty hours of training per week. Bunnies were required to be able to identify more than one hundred brands of liquor and be skilled in garnishing twenty cocktail variations.

The Bunny Hutch was a nightclub located near the lobby. © Bill Frantz

Jerry Pawlak rose through the ranks at the Lake Geneva Playboy Club-Hotel. He would eventually become maître d', which involved working with big-name entertainers, welcoming guests, assigning tables, and supervising the waitstaff.

As part of the training they needed to know the "Bunny Stance," the "Bunny Perch," and the "Bunny Dip," the various ways to stand, sit, and serve drinks, requiring intricate hip, leg, and back movements. In addition to glasses of Scotch, whiskey, bourbon, rye, blended cocktails, wine, beer, and ice cream drinks, a typical service tray held several ashtrays, a tip tray, and a stack of cocktail napkins. Four pens hung off the right hip, for signatures on guest checks. The service tray was held by the left hand, with the right over the left hip, while balancing on three-inch satin pump heels. Obviously, this was not a job for the weak. Bunnies worked a maximum forty hours a week, being paid $2.01 an hour. They relied heavily on tips, which could be lucrative if one was an excellent, attentive server.

Demerits were given if a bunny's appearance was not up to snuff. Bunny Mothers ran a tight ship. First there was Bev Russell, then came Ann Hamilton Baran, Ursula Wieman and Gail Hintz Frantz. At age twenty-three, Frantz was the youngest Bunny Mother, starting as a Bunny herself at age eighteen on June 6, 1968, two weeks after the Club-Hotel opened. When she broke her arm and became Ann's assistant, Gail learned the intricacies of managing 125 bunnies. She recovered and went back to work on the floor until the fall of 1973, taking over as a "Mother," when Ursula left the resort. Frantz went on to be Corporate Trainer for Playboy Hotels, with her offices in Lake Geneva. She returned as Bunny Mother in 1978, holding that position until the Club-Hotel closed. She married Playboy photographer Bill Frantz in 1978, in a ceremony at the ski chalet presided over by a local judge. Like most of the bunnies, Gail fondly remembers her Playboy experiences, recalling that it was a "fabulous company to work for."

The Playboy Bunny outfit was the first service uniform registered with the United States Patent and Trademark Office (U.S. trademark registration number 0762884). Renee Blot, working with Chicago corset maker Kabo, perfected the look in 1962. The firm came up with a corseted, one-piece outfit made from a rayon-satin material. Two of the resort's seamstresses

CONTINUED ON PAGE 49

ABOVE: Promotional photos, such as this one taken in the golf clubhouse, aligned the Playboy brand with the resort's many amenities. © Bill Frantz BELOW: Bunnies Kim and Marion were two local girls selected to work at the resort.

Sandy Farwell worked at Playboy from May 1968 to the resort's closing in 1982. Courtesy of Sandy Farwell.

Sandy's Story

Sandy Farwell worked at the Playboy Club-Hotel from its opening on May 4, 1968, to the closing in March of 1982. Farwell started at age 21, newly married and living in Rockford, Illinois. Before her Playboy career, she was a secretary. Farwell's husband, Bill, suggested she apply for the job after seeing an advertisement in a local newspaper. The notice indicated that a new Playboy resort was scheduled to open soon and that the resort was looking for girls to be "glamorous Playboy bunnies."

Bunnies had to be between eighteen and twenty-five, with their weight in proportion to their height. Since the Lake Geneva Playboy Club-Hotel was still under construction, interviews were held at the nearby Abbey Resort in Fontana. As instructed, Farwell brought a bathing suit. She was interviewed by Hefner's longtime Chicago nightclub manager, John Dante. He praised her legs and asked if her husband would be jealous of her working at Playboy. She laughed and replied that Bill was the one who suggested she try out. During that first week or so after getting the job, Farwell came home tired and crying, with bleeding feet. She lost twenty pounds the first month.

But it got easier and she went on to work in the Penthouse, waiting on Hefner at the grand opening and then regularly waiting on him when he visited Lake Geneva. She emphasized that Hefner "was a nice man, very respectful." She even went to a party at his Chicago mansion, just to say she had been to one of his soirees. She met Sonny & Cher, Bob Hope and Sammy Davis, Jr.

Sandy later returned to Grand Geneva as concierge. She subsequently worked at Grand Geneva from its opening in 1994 until retiring October 30, 2011.

A Bunny Tale

Left to right: Bunny Danielle, Bunny Peg, and Bunny Vanett.

necessary. The dorm was located just off the second hole of The Brute golf course. The bunnies would watch the curious golfers driving around and around the building, hoping to catch a glimpse of a real, live bunny. Some duffers even stopped and peered through the fence. As Weber says, "The funny thing is that these male golfers never understood that we could hear their conversations from the tee. Needless to say that none of us were very friendly when they attempted to make conversation or asked for us to return their golf balls when they directly aimed for our building."

The bunnies had certain privileges that other employees did not enjoy. They parked closer to the hotel and could be picked up by the bell staff or were allowed to drive through the front gate. However, permission was required to sit with a male, even one's father. There was no touching

Pegs Weber was introduced to the idea of working for Playboy through her mother, who had seen an ad in a Milwaukee newspaper indicating that the company was hosting a "Bunny Hunt." Weber had been working at the Tracks tavern/restaurant in Milwaukee and had plenty of serving experience. She remembers being asked to wear a one-piece swimsuit and high heels at the audition. Bunny Mother Gail Frantz conducted her interview, launching a longtime friendship.

After her costume fittings, Weber began working at the club in May of 1981, chaperoned by her mother. She moved into the bunny dorm, noting the building's surrounding security fencing. She soon learned why it was

allowed, and it was an understood rule that the tail was especially off-limits. It didn't matter if a customer was disrespectful, drunk, or loud, bunnies did not tolerate any bad behavior. Out-of-line guests were handed their bill and had to pay it promptly before being escorted out. "End of conversation! It was great. You truly didn't have to take it," says Weber.

Bunny Mother Gail Frantz (front) managed 125 bunnies at the Lake Geneva Playboy Club-Hotel. © Bill Frantz

A bunny bartender mixes cocktails for a corporate event. © Bill Frantz

CONTINUED FROM PAGE 43

individually sized each costume. Each woman's uniform was selected by the Bunny Mother, who chose the colors according to what she considered a match for that particular bunny's personality. It took an average of three fittings for each bunny before the uniform was complete. Since the costume's bra was a standard D cup, many of the women were "stuffed" to achieve a better cleavage. One of the seamstresses, Pat Moorhouse, still works in Lake Geneva.

If a bunny put on five extra pounds, she had a week to trim back or be written up with a disciplinary note. If she didn't lose the plumpness by the ensuing week, she was forbidden to work.

For each shift, Bunny Mother Gail Frantz made sure that tails were appropriately fluffed, nails manicured, and seams straight. Adjustable satin bunny ears, cotton tails, collars with bow ties, cuffs with links, pantyhose, and matching high-heeled shoes completed the look. Learning to dress was a task. Bunnies wore Danskin support stockings, either in nude or in black. Each bunny wore a name tag on a satin rosette pinned over the right hip bone so it could be read by seated guests. Many bunnies used stage names on their tags. Pam Ellis, using her middle name, was called Bunny Jo, and later earned the nickname of Jo-Jo, which she still uses.

The locker room where bunnies prepped themselves was a theater with bright lights, cluttered counter tops, and lots of chairs. Dramatic makeovers happened daily. The women had to be perfect, wearing false eyelashes and heavy makeup, their nails painted, their shoes polished. The women worked three- to four-hour shifts, winding down around 1 a.m. or so. Many worked double shifts.

The Rule Book

The bunny manual spelled out the do's and don'ts of working at the clubs and resorts under the Playboy mantle. The booklet indicated that the bunny has "become what the Ziegfield girl was to another generation, synonymous with the most glamorous young women in the world." Finder's fees were given out to bunnies for referring other applicants who were eventually hired. The incentive system included a daily Good Service contest, where a bunny earned merit points and a choice of shifts.

Under the rules, bunnies were not permitted to chew gum or eat while on duty, nor could they drink alcoholic beverages in the Club-Hotel at any time. They were not allowed soft drinks, lemonade, or even water in view of keyholders and guests, but could have a nonalcoholic drink behind the scenes.

Demerits were given if the bunny ears were not worn in the center of the head or bent incorrectly, improper makeup, not doing the Bunny dip, or not changing ashtrays.

Bunnies worked all over the resort, in many different colorful costumes. They could pose for photos provided there was no physical contact with guests. Top photo courtesy of Susan Rapach Hayunga.

Memorabilia from the Lake Geneva Playboy Club-Hotel has been loaned or donated to Grand Geneva over the years. The green bunny ears belong to former bunny Sandy Farwell.

Bunnies were not to mix with guests; however, they could pose for pictures with patrons providing there was no physical contact. The women could also dance with patrons at parties, but only if there was no touching. Acceptable dances included the Twist, the Watusi, and the Bugaloo.

The manual went on to encourage the proper use of makeup, "an invaluable aid in bunny beauty." The Bunny Mother and the Club's Cosmetic Bunny were there to coach and assist with the extra touches. Skillful eye makeup included use of shadow and false eyelashes, with lipstick being "bright, vivid, and highlighted with gloss" to avoid a washed-out look.

To relieve tired feet, Bunnies were encouraged to roll their feet over an empty cola bottle, or soak them in a solution of epsom salt and warm water for a half hour, then elevate the feet. Hose were to be rinsed in cold water and refrigerated before wearing.

The Beginning of The End

When the Playboy Club-Hotel first opened, Hefner said, "I'm overwhelmed by it all myself." This feeling might have been a premonition because by the early 1980s, the ever-expanding Playboy empire itself was becoming "overwhelmed." It was over-extended financially and was ultimately overtaken by events that seemed beyond its control. The London casino was the only real moneymaker in the chain. When that site lost its gambling license in October 1981 and subsequently closed, the Playboy party was over.

According to its managers, the Lake Geneva Playboy Club-Hotel was still profitable; however, Playboy's overall cash outflow was too much. The entire Playboy resort and hotel operation lost $5.2 million in 1981 and the decision was made to close the door on the accommodations area of the operation. On Friday, November 20, 1981, Derick J. Daniels, president of Playboy Enterprises, announced the completion of a cash deal of $42 million, selling the Great Gorge and Lake Geneva sites to Americana Hotels and a partnership of Eugene Golub, William B. Kaplan, and Van L. Pell, executives of the Chicago-based Romanek Golub Co. The deal took effect December 31, 1981.

Hefner brought in former newspaper executive Daniels to train Christie Hefner to take over the Playboy domain and to turn around the company. With the resorts out of the way, Daniels emphasized that Playboy was going to concentrate on its magazine publishing, cable television, and franchising products.

The familiar welcoming signs at the entrance were dismantled and removed on Wednesday March 24, 1982. With that, it was officially over. After almost fourteen years, the Lake Geneva Playboy Club-Hotel closed forever.

Christie Hefner

DID YOU EVER WANT TO BE A PLAYBOY BUNNY OR WANT TO WORK AT THE PLAYBOY CLUB-HOTEL IN LAKE GENEVA?
I worked as an Assistant Bunny Mother at the Boston Playboy Club, the summer of 1971. I went many times to the Lake Geneva resort from the time I started at the company in November of 1975 through to when we sold the property.

DID YOU DRIVE UP, USE A LIMO, OR FLY TO WISCONSIN WHEN VISITING THE PROPERTY?
I mostly drove up to Lake Geneva, but I did once fly up (in a thunderstorm) with a colleague in his small plane. I had my high school (New Trier West) graduation party (in lieu of a prom) in Lake Geneva and the class took a train up and back, spending the day on the property in the spring of 1970.

DO YOU HAVE ANY STORIES ABOUT MEETING ENTERTAINERS?
I loved the VIP room and loved the shows. I was there when Sonny & Cher performed, and Chastity and Cher mingled among the guests, both in bunny costumes.

WAS THE RESORT HUGH HEFNER'S FAVORITE AMONG ALL HIS VARIOUS PROPERTIES?
Hef loved the Lake Geneva property both because it was one of the company's first resorts, and it was so beautifully designed.

WERE YOU INVOLVED IN THE DECISIONS TO CLOSE THE RESORTS?
As a member of the Playboy board of directors, I was involved in the decision to sell the hotels and resorts. Overall, that line of business was not profitable for the company, and it made sense to sell it off.

DID YOU EVER RETURN TO STAY OR VISIT THE AMERICANA? HAVE YOU BEEN BACK TO GRAND GENEVA?
The original purchaser put little investment into the property, but the Grand Geneva people have been wonderful owners. I have been back with my mother and step-father when I was still playing golf to play a round and have dinner several times.

The No-Name Sculpture

Charles Moelter, at left, poses with his sculpture in 1969.

When guests observe the enormous untitled sculpture on the 16th tee of The Brute golf course, they often ask, "What is it?" A frustrated golfer? An animal? Part of the human anatomy?

According to sculptor and Lake Geneva resident Charles Moelter, the answer is yes to all of the above. "Use your imagination," he says. "It is still titillating minds and that is what it was meant to do."

An alumnus from the Art Institute of Chicago, Moelter was a building contractor in the 1960s, working for Playboy in Chicago. His father owned a farm just a mile from Lake Geneva. When the Lake Geneva Playboy Club-Hotel was nearly complete, execs invited several artists to the hotel, seeking original sculpture submissions. The winning pieces would be placed around the resort. Playboy Vice President Arnold Morton knew Moelter from his contracting work in Chicago, and invited Moelter to be part of the group.

Moelter presented an abstract model that would double as a rain shelter. He presented a sketch of his artwork, built models, and even posed one on the golf course and photographed it with the hotel in the background.

His submission was accepted, and he was paid roughly $25,000 to build the structure in the summer of 1969.

It was an interesting challenge, he says. First a floating foundation was built to accommodate the unstable ground. Then he built the steel structure and covered it with galvanized wire and cement. Moelter was worried about golfers from larger tournaments climbing on it, so he built it to support 200 people standing on top of it. It was completed in three months.

Moelter is now retired on his family farm near Grand Geneva. "At the time, it was a big deal," he says of being chosen to create the golf course work of art. "It's a no-name sculpture, I guess. You have to use your imagination."

Rock & Roll in the Country

PLAYBOY BUILDS A WORLD-CLASS RECORDING STUDIO

VISITORS TO LAKE GENEVA are often surprised to learn that the area once boasted a world-class music recording studio. Despite the string of hits this studio produced, it remains an underappreciated piece of local history. Even those familiar with it have difficulty telling the story completely.

Performers who passed through Lake Geneva included some of the industry's biggest names: John Mellencamp, Survivor, T'Pau, Cheap Trick, Guns N' Roses, Bon Jovi, Adrian Belew, Robert Plant, Enuff Z'nuff, Crash Test Dummies, Nine Inch Nails, Live, Red Hot Chili Peppers, and many more. All of these artists at one time or another recorded music in what is now an engineering office at Grand Geneva Resort & Spa.

Bun E. Carlos is the drummer for Cheap Trick, a world-renowned rock band that formed in Rockford, Illinois, in the late 1960s and went on to record several top-ten hits and platinum-selling albums. They recorded their 1985 album, *Standing on the Edge*, at the Lake Geneva studio.

"It wasn't that they put a studio in there that was surprising," he says. "[The surprise was] that it was as good as it was."

The Lake Geneva studio proved popular with musicians, but it struggled financially, despite producing three platinum albums — by Live, Nine Inch Nails and Crash Test Dummies — in its final days.

A Proposal for Playboy

Andy Waterman grew up in Dundee, a suburb northwest of Chicago. A gifted musician, he frequently ventured north across the state line to play gigs in Lake Geneva.

Then a Chicago audio supplier told him about Vern and Jan Castle, the husband-wife owners of Castle Recording in Lake Geneva. The Castles were retired, and though they weren't household names, they'd made a good living as an opening act for big-name entertainers. In their garage recording studio, they recorded mostly radio commercials.

The Royal Recorders studio, pictured here in 1986, was outfitted with the best equipment in the industry. Photo courtesy of Ron Fajerstein

ABOVE: Shade Tree co-owner Andy Waterman worked with Grammy-nominated jazz vocalist Judy Roberts on several of her albums. Judy also performed regularly at the Lake Geneva Playboy Club-Hotel. © Bill Frantz
BELOW: According to Royal Recorders studio owner Ron Fajerstein, Guns N' Roses recorded some vocal overdubs in Lake Geneva for their albums *Use Your Illusion 1* and *Use Your Illusion 2*. As the story goes, Axl Rose bought a ten-acre plot of land here. But before he built a house, he and wife Erin Everly called it quits. The property was sold in 1998. © WireImages

Some of those ads, written for brands like Wrigley's, Menards, and American Family Insurance, are still played today.

Waterman took a job at Castle; he produced, engineered, sang, and picked up an instrument when a jingle called for it. On the side, he picked up a gig with the house band at Lake Geneva's Playboy Club-Hotel. At least once a week, he'd don a tux and head up to Playboy, filling in for sick or touring musicians.

Playboy provided the perfect venue for top-name entertainment. In 1977, Waterman had been in Lake Geneva for about three years and lobbied Playboy to expand their entertainment even further.

Top artists of the day were performing at Playboy. Rock stars appearing at nearby Alpine Valley, one of the nation's largest outdoor music venues, would also stay at the resort. The region, Waterman thought, was ripe with a captive market. He hoped to capitalize on that and introduce the country to the thriving Midwestern music scene.

So Waterman proposed that Playboy build a recording studio, the only one its clubs were ever known to have. In just three short weeks, after meetings with Playboy suits and an audience with Hefner's daughter, Christie, the studio got a green light. Adjacent to its massive convention center, Playboy constructed a thirty-five-by-twenty-five-foot recording studio. "I'm almost positive [Playboy's] investment was just under $60,000 to build the shell," he says. "We were to pay $2,500 a month in rent to them. At that time, we could bill that in two days."

Optimism Runs High

Waterman doesn't remember the day Shade Tree Studios officially opened, but pegs it in early 1978. A story in the March 4 edition of *Billboard* that year alerted the industry to the new space, and the studio, with its state-of-the-art MCI 528 automated console, quickly booked up. Even though Waterman was by this point seriously in debt, nobody was nervous, least of all Playboy.

For a while, the deals weren't hard to bring in. Judy Roberts, a famed Chicago jazz artist, recorded here. John Mellencamp, Matrix, and Sweetbottom also laid tracks at Shade Tree. In addition to the recording studio, Shade Tree formed a production company to scout and promote new artists.

But problems began when the economy took a turn for the worse and record labels began to slash studio budgets.

"It changed directions," remembers Larry Schroeder, also a studio stakeholder. "They were introducing cassettes and videos. [Recording] budgets that were $180,000 were down to $73,000, and you're still constantly updating your equipment and you're not billing what you were. When you did the math, it just didn't look very good."

Schroeder doesn't remember what day he finally surrendered to the bottom line, only that he did. "I just left it," he says. "I just walked away from it."

Sound Summit

In 1982, Playboy also walked away, selling its Lake Geneva compound. As Americana Resort took over, Shade Tree Studios remained dormant.

At some point, the late Phil Bonanno decided to revive Shade Tree. Jim Bartz, a musician and audio engineer now living in Seattle, started his career here. Shade Tree, he explains, became Sound Summit.

"It was 1985 that I started working there," he says. "It wasn't a world-class studio until it became Sound Summit. Then it got a Neve 8068 console. It was a rock and roll paradise. That's a very coveted board. I was told it was the actual console John Lennon recorded Double Fantasy on. It had, like, a pedigree to it."

Sound Summit, he adds, was Bonanno's "brainchild," funded with money he'd made as a producer for bands, including Survivor. Bonanno also had partners. Julie (Whowell) Ieronimo was a receptionist there, and believes that while Bonanno did have a stake in the studio, a group of investors on the West Coast were the majority shareholders.

"Sound Summit was owned by a group of dentists, who I never met, from Van Nuys, California," she explains, still shocked by the idea. "That's what I remember being told. I never met them, but that's where our paychecks were from."

During that time, tax laws specific to record-making made studios a great shelter. It's possible, sources speculate, the investor group cared little about the music and simply wanted a place to store cash.

Bonanno's connections in the music industry brought in bands like Survivor, Cheap Trick, and Skid Row. But frequently, the studio was used to record or mix only a few songs and not booked for the extended periods of time that would help it remain in the black.

In the summer of 1985, recalls Ieronimo, studio staff was informed that the majority investors had pulled out. "The paychecks stopped coming," she says, "and we all walked out. I couldn't believe it."

Royal Recorders

Ron Fajerstein loves music. He loves it so much that 29 years ago, he walked into Sound Summit and decided to take the biggest risk of his life. His family had made millions in the diamond import business and, unlike the dentists, he wasn't looking for a tax shelter. He wanted to make music, and he wanted to partner with people like Phil Bonanno who knew the business. Looking

ABOVE: Diamond importer Ron Fajerstein, on the left, transformed Sound Summit into Royal Recorders. He's shown here with Adrian Belew, famous in the 1970s and 1980s for his work with Frank Zappa, David Bowie, and Talking Heads. BELOW: Fajerstein invested significantly into the best studio equipment available.

© Bill Frantz

back, he realizes that he was in over his head almost from the start.

In the UK, Fajerstein met Helen Tyler, who was an assistant studio manager at Battery Studios. "There was a really large console, Sound Studio Logic made the console, and Battery was on the cutting edge and had it at the time," recalls Tyler. "Ron being Ron wanted the biggest and the best in the studio he was building."

Tyler led Fajerstein on his Battery tour, and not only did he end up committing to the eighty-input SSL, he offered Tyler, still somewhat green in her mid 20s, a job as Royal Recorders' studio manager.

Out of Control
In addition to outfitting the studio with the best equipment available, Fajerstein also sank a small fortune into a stretch Rolls Royce limo for visiting bands. At the same time, his production company was scouring the globe on his expense account, looking for new talent.

Bands like T'Pau (produced by Roy Thomas Baker), Nine Inch Nails, Skid

Row, and Enuff Z'nuff all recorded here, and turned out albums that sold millions. But in the end, the money it took to get bands to Lake Geneva was greater than the money the studio earned.

Eventually, Fajerstein reached a point where he decided he could no longer hemorrhage cash in the name of music. Sometime in the early 1990s, he sold the studio to two of its engineers under a land contract. Under new management, Live's *Throwing Copper* album was recorded here and sold nine million copies. Crash Test Dummies recorded *God Shuffled His Feet* almost entirely here; it reached triple platinum status.

Then the phone just stopped ringing. Seeing there was no hope, the engineers gave the studio back to Fajerstein.

Trying to recoup some of his investment, Fajerstein dismantled the beloved eighty-input SSL console, the true heartbeat of the studio, and sent it to a studio in Texas. He says it now resides in the basement studio of Chicago-based R & B artist and producer R. Kelly.

Music Makers Remember

"It wasn't that they put a studio in there that was surprising. That it was as good as it was, [that was] the surprise."

- Bun E. Carlos, Cheap Trick drummer, who recorded *Standing on the Edge* and the *Top Gun* soundtrack at Sound Summit Studio, the successor to Shade Tree.

"It was a gigantic candy land, all that audio gear . . . I always made a great living in the industry, but I just couldn't make a living as a studio owner."

- Rich Denhart, studio engineer with Royal Recorders, who eventually bought the studio with engineer Dan Harjung and renamed it Musichead.

"I remember The Beach Boys were playing at Alpine Valley and they came in to work on a song, and Brian Wilson sat down on the couch and we talked for three hours. He was so nice."

- Julie (Whowell) Ieronimo, studio receptionist during its reign as Sound Summit and Royal Recorders.

"It was great while it lasted. It was special. I believe that, for me, it helped my creativity to be in that atmosphere. I'm not a big city person to begin with and I loved living there. The studio was fully state-of-the-art and there was hardly a better studio anywhere."

- Adrian Belew, a world-renowned guitarist discovered by Frank Zappa, who toured with David Bowie and The Talking Heads, and produced several of his own acclaimed albums at Royal Recorders.

[During the Americana days] the rooms in the hotel had 1970's eight-track clock

Woody Herman's band recorded here in 1978. © Bill Frantz

radios, including old eight track tapes to play in them. The carpets were shag, bright orange, and the wallpaper was brown and gold stripes. Nothing had changed since Hugh's days. It was a bit like "The Shining" out there, but without the snow. It was an unforgettable time, and I remember details of making that record (God Shuffled His Feet) like it was yesterday.

—Brad Roberts, Band Member, Crash Test Dummies

The happiest times of my career were the years I spent performing at the Lake Geneva Playboy Club-Hotel with my jazz quartet. Not only was it a first-class gig (in the Playmate Bar) but the whole essence of Hugh Hefner's posh and sophisticated operation was like no other. Another amazing thing was the fact that there was a recording studio on the property. After our gig at the Playmate Bar, we would walk over and work on our album until daylight. The atmosphere of being peacefully secluded in beautiful Lake Geneva, in combination with all the perks of a world-class, high-tech studio, was the best ever. My first three albums featured original songs by the Playboy Club-Hotel house pianist, the late Russ Long. I went on to have a No. 1 hit song in 1980, a song recorded at Shade Tree Studios in wonderful Lake Geneva. What a blessing!

—Judy Roberts, Musician

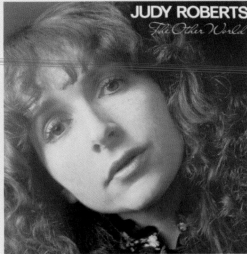

Courtesy of Sony Music Archives

Timeline

"I can certainly see the logic in it, but the acts that were coming to Playboy and Alpine were there on a weekend basis, not establishing any kind of residency and not long-term. Would I have supported it as a concept? Yes. Do I think it was a good concept in hindsight? Probably not."

— Dan Stone, vice president for clubs and hotels with Playboy Enterprises, who admits he was unaware of the studio's existence until contacted for this book.

Castle Recording
1960s – 1980s

Owned by Vern and Jan Castle, the home studio on the south shore of Geneva Lake is a destination for many Chicago musicians. Several popular advertising jingles for companies like Menards and American Family Insurance are recorded in this studio. In 1979, the Castles record *Everything Old Is New Again*, which goes on to earn a Grammy nomination. Andy Waterman, a jack-of-all-trades at Castle and a teen jingle prodigy buys Castle Recording and moves much of it to the Lake Geneva Playboy Club-Hotel. Castle continues to record jingles, but Waterman wants to tap into what he sees as a thriving Midwestern music scene he feels the rest of the country is ignoring.

Shade Tree
1978 – 1982

With his wife, Judy, and Larry Schroeder, a local businessman with a music store and ties to big finance, Waterman talks the Lake Geneva Playboy Club-Hotel and its executives, including Christie Hefner, into building the shell of a studio and leasing it to him. In addition to working at Castle, Waterman also subs in Playboy's house band. Waterman and his wife divorce in 1980, and he leaves Shade Tree. Schroeder says he's unsure how long he tried to keep the studio alive. Credits can be found as late as 1982. Recording artists include:

- John Cougar Mellencamp
- Sweetbottom
- Matrix
- Judy Roberts

Courtesy of Sony Music Archives

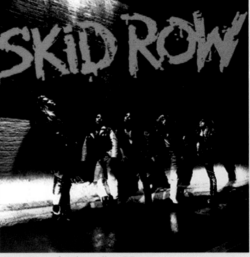
Courtesy of Adrenaline PR

Courtesy of Sony Music Archives

Sound Summit
1984 – 1986

Phil Bonanno purchases the former Shade Tree and renames the studio Sound Summit. A producer and engineer who found success touring with bands like Survivor, he opens up shop with capital from a group of investors, including a group of dentists from Van Nuys, California, according to a former staff member. While the studio is used by major artists, it isn't usually booked for entire albums. The recording or mixing of only a few tracks on an album doesn't allow the studio to remain in the black. Bonanno dies in 2007; his engineering credits include albums for Styx, Enuff Z'nuff, Cheap Trick, and Dennis DeYoung. Recording artists at Sound Summit include:

- Survivor
- Cheap Trick – *Standing on the Edge* (entire album)

Royal Recorders
1986 – 1992

Diamond importer Ron Fajerstein, a self-described "frustrated musician," buys Sound Summit and renames it Royal Recorders. Fajerstein would be the studio's longest and most-heavily invested owner. The equipment value alone was said to be in excess of $500,000 and a stretch Rolls Royce limo used by visiting artists

at the time carried a six-figure price tag. His separate management company also toured the world looking for the next big musical act. For a time, he managed Enuff Z'nuff. Fajerstein eventually sold the studio on a land contract to audio engineers Dan Harjung and Rich Denhart. Recording artists include:

- T'Pau – *Bridge of Spies*
- Robert Plant (formerly of Led Zeppelin)
- Adrian Belew
- Guns N' Roses
- Skid Row
- Nine Inch Nails
- Red Hot Chili Peppers
- Top Gun Soundtrack – "Mighty Wings"

Musichead
1992 – 1994

Engineers Dan Harjung and Rich Denhart buy the studio. Using their audio-know-how and industry connections, they score some impressive credits for the studio, but ultimately, says Harjung, "the phone just stopped ringing." Recording artists include:

- Live – *Throwing Copper* (mixed at Musichead)
- Crash Test Dummies – *God Shuffled His Feet*

A New Direction

THE PLAYBOY CLUB-HOTEL IS TRANSFORMED INTO AMERICANA RESORT

THE PLAYBOY CLUBS remained a part of the American landscape for two decades. But by the early 1980s, changing tastes and poor financial performance forced the end of Playboy's foray into hospitality, including its Lake Geneva resort.

According to news reports at the time, Playboy Enterprises was "badly overextended." While a handful of the clubs were profitable, they only accounted for a small portion of the company's overall bottom line. And by the late 1970s, Playboy was no longer a trendsetter in sex, sophistication, or entertainment. Derick J. Daniels, president of Playboy Enterprises, offered this statement to the media upon the sale of the Lake Geneva club in late 1981:

"Over the past year, the company has been reassessing its lines of business and focusing on those where we have established strength. The sale of the resorts is one further step in the ongoing process. We are redeploying our assets and accelerating our efforts in the areas where we have proven capabilities — magazine publishing, cable television, programming, and licensing the Playboy name and trademark worldwide."

Americana Takes Over

At the end of 1981, Playboy sold its Lake Geneva club including all of their land holdings to the Americana Hotels Corp., a Chicago-based hospitality group. They purchased the Lake Geneva club and another Playboy club, Great Gorge in McAfee, New Jersey, for a cash deal of $42 million. Tax records show the Lake Geneva property accounted for $11.95 million of the deal.

As quickly as the bunnies had appeared in southern Wisconsin, they hopped out again. All evidence of the Club's Playboy past was swept away under the new management.

Before Marcus took ownership in 1994, the property operated as Americana Resort. Today the grounds are meticulously cared for, with views of the countryside from the lake view rooms.

ABOVE: On March 24, 1982, the last remnants of the Playboy era were removed. Courtesy of the *Lake Geneva Regional News*.

Local media reported that while the new owners would keep the physical property "mostly unchanged," they were ushering in a "new image of family respectability."

The Living Room Restaurant became Annie's Country Kitchen. The Playmate Bar was now the Steakhouse and Saloon.

Overseeing all of the changes was Wisconsin native Robert Butschke, Americana's general manager. "We took over the property on March 17 (1982)," Butschke recalls of his arrival at the former Playboy Club-Hotel. "There were 720 employees . . . and we terminated 720 and rehired 220. That became known as Black Tuesday. . . . That was a very dramatic time because it really affected the people that were there."

Butschke and the other Americana management worked to repackage Hugh Hefner's vision. "I can tell you this much, I found it very interesting going through the

The Americana sign stood at the entrance from 1982 to 1993.
© Bill Frantz

bunny dorm," says Butschke, pausing to laugh even after all of these years. "We were going to turn it into employee housing and it was a complete mess. The most striking thing to me is the amount of money [bunnies] must have spent on toenail and fingernail polish because it was all over the place."

Rebranding to Attract Corporate Business

Cleaning up spilled nail polish wasn't Butschke's biggest challenge though. Attracting new business and increasing slumping occupancy rates ranked first on his to-do list. Butschke says that when he took over the Playboy property for Americana, the Abbey Resort ranked first in attracting conventions and conferences, Lake Lawn Resort was second, and Playboy came in a woeful third, despite its 1,000-plus acres, 300-plus rooms, and bounty of amenities.

"The major thing about my stay at that property," he reflects, "is that we took it from the image of Playboy, which limited many corporations from doing business

Grand Geneva's sweeping Prairie-style gateway greets guests to the resort today.

Annie's Country Kitchen, an Americana Resort restaurant, was best known for its extravagant Sunday brunch. © Bill Frantz

there, to opening the door to anyone. It became more family and corporate-oriented than it had been. A lot of your major Fortune 500 companies at the time did not really cherish the thought of holding annual meetings at a Playboy resort. That image did not fit well with families."

According to many people who worked there at the time, room occupancy rates started strong at the beginning of Americana's reign. For three years, says Butschke, Americana's fortunes in Lake Geneva rose. When he came on, he says gross revenue for Playboy was just under $3 million a year. By 1985, the resort had quadrupled that amount and Americana "had put a big hurt" on the Abbey and Lake Lawn "by the business we stole and the business we retained with the service we provided."

"We had a gross revenue of $12 million and were turning a profit of twenty-five percent," Butschke says. "That was an amazing turn-around."

Dave Hallenbeck is the director of golf operations for Grand Geneva Resort & Spa and has been on property for forty years. "The beginning years of Americana were very successful," he agrees. "Bob Butschke and his management team helped breathe life into the property after it was purchased by Americana. In fact, our second season in the golf operation set an all-time record in both rounds and revenues. We saw familiar faces return and the property saw a new energy during those early 80s."

Singer John Denver and his father would fly in on their private plane and play a few rounds. Baseball legend Mickey Mantle hit the links here. So, too, did NFL running backs O.J. Simpson, Gale Sayers, and Jim Brown. Major League Baseball Players from the Brewers, the Cubs, and the White Sox could also be found on the courses.

Falling into Disrepair

Unfortunately the turn-around didn't last. Ultimately, Butschke was sent to manage the Great Gorge property in New Jersey. He was later asked to form a management company (Key Wisconsin) and take over operations of both Great Gorge and Lake Geneva.

While he did so gladly, he was limited in what he could achieve as a non-owner. Butschke says capital was initially made available to refurbish and maintain the Lake Geneva property, but it became harder to raise the necessary money as time went on. He says

From Playboy's Living Room Restaurant to Americana's Annie's Country Kitchen to Grand Geneva's Grand Cafe.

By the mid-1980s Americana fell into financial trouble and the property began to decline. © Bill Frantz

Americana invested only about $3 million into maintenance and upgrades at the aging resort. What once had been a world-class facility fell into decline.

Like the ski area, the resort's golf courses, Hallenbeck says, managed to stay alive during the later Americana years. "The downfall was when funding from corporate stopped flowing in and the physical nature of it deteriorated. We pretty much limped by on next to nothing, but we did it."

Americana's Final Chapter

Celebrity golfers and rock and roll couldn't keep the resort alive, though. Americana officially entered foreclosure in 1986, but remained open. It then sold to an interim partnership for $5.7 million. By 1988, according to news reports, Chicago's JMB Realty Corp. had sealed a deal to become the resort's newest owner for a cool $6.5 million. JMB executives kept the Americana name and possibly believed they could achieve significant profits without much capital outlay. They were quickly proved wrong. Within a few years, Americana became a summer-only resort, with many of its rooms sealed off.

In 1992, JMB folded and put Americana up for auction. By that time, Americana lacked an identity or customer base. Roofs leaked and deferred maintenance was visible in every corner of the hotel. The building was literally falling apart, a reality that scared off many potential buyers. Almost every hotel chain in the country considered purchasing the property but almost all determined that the property was beyond repair. The investment appeared to be a losing proposition.

The minimum bid was set at $10 million. According to news reports from the *Chicago Tribune*, the only bid came in at half that. By 1993, when it was rescued by Marcus Hotels, the property resembled a ghost town. Marcus paid just $4.25 million, one-third of what Playboy sold it for in 1981.

"Marcus had a lot to do," says one former manager, "but they knew it and they were ready for it."

Hallenbeck, the forty-year property veteran, marvels that he's still around. "I honestly thought the place would be closed and grassed-in, and a plaque would go up. But that didn't happen. The surprising element was the vision Marcus brought in."

The Geneva Club, a private lounge, now stands near the center of the main lodge, offering casual and business seating complete with workstations, reading materials, and games.

The Marcus Years

ONE FAMILY'S VISION CREATES THE GRAND GENEVA RESORT & SPA

IN 1935, A POLISH IMMIGRANT NAMED BEN MARCUS decided to capitalize on his love of American Westerns by opening a one-screen movie house in Ripon, Wisconsin. By 1996, Marcus had built his corporation into one of the largest motel chains in the United States, the nineteenth largest theater circuit, and the largest Kentucky Fried Chicken franchisee in the Midwest. The company has continued its growth into resorts and other avenues of business.

Marcus was an entrepreneurial youth; his numerous ventures included joining his father's cattle brokering business and operating a paper route for the *Minneapolis Journal* before moving on to the newspaper's circulation, advertising, and entertainment staffs. Building on his experience at the *Journal*, Marcus then began working as a marketing manager for the local movie theaters. He developed marketing promotions, wrote advertisements, and assisted with movie selection. By 1935, he decided to go into business for himself and opened his movie theater in Ripon, purchasing a burned-out department store building.

Borrowing money from his family and securing a bank loan, Marcus transformed the building into a state-of-the-art facility called The Campus Theater (due to its proximity to Ripon College). It opened on November 1, 1935, with a showing of the film *It's in the Air*, starring Comedian Jack Benny. The theater was a success, and soon Marcus was able to purchase a theater in Tomah as well. Within a few years, Marcus had turned his love of movies into a successful chain, building and purchasing several theaters throughout Wisconsin.

After building his business from just one movie theater to hundreds of movie screens, restaurants, and hotel properties, Ben Marcus retired in 1991. His son, Steve, took over and later led the efforts to purchase the property that would become Grand Geneva Resort & Spa.

Expanding and diversifying his empire, Marcus invested in a meat packing firm, a film distributorship, a popcorn and candy vendor, several real estate development companies, and the Big Boy chain of restaurants. Marcus's first Big Boy opened in 1958, and within four years, he owned another six of the popular burger franchises. In 1960, Marcus discovered Colonel Sanders' Original Recipe Kentucky Fried Chicken (at that time a secret recipe that was franchised to independent restaurants) and began featuring that dish at all of his Marc's Big Boy restaurants. That same year, Marcus also expanded his business empire into the mid-price motel market by opening the first of his Guest House Inns.

The Next Generation

In 1991, Ben Marcus, who built a nationwide corporation from just one movie theater, officially retired and named his son board chairman. By 1993, the firm launched a $180 million, three-year plan to add twenty-five new company-owned Budgetels, fifty new movie screens and several new Applebee's family restaurants, a new franchise opportunity that Marcus had entered in 1990.

With a strongly established history in the hospitality business, the Marcus Corporation was primed to expand its hotel and resort portfolio in the 1990s. When the Americana Resort in Lake Geneva came up for sale, the Marcus Corporation was a strong potential buyer.

Lee Berthelsen and Michael Hool of Marcus Hotels toured the Americana site and despite the derelict condition, they recognized the property's possibilities. Ben's son, Steve, appreciated the beauty of the property and its Frank Lloyd Wright-inspired architecture. Marcus loved the gently rolling landscape and the potential for remaking the resort into a premier holiday getaway. He saw the run-down condition of the property as a challenge, but not an insurmountable one.

The two firms reached an agreement in 1993. The Marcus Corporation purchased the Americana property from LGA Associates, an affiliate of JMB Realty, for a rumored $4.25 million, far lower than JMB had hoped. In a newspaper interview on July 15, 1993, Berthelsen promised that Marcus was going to "restore, renovate, and enhance" the resort and all its facilities. Work would commence in the fall of that year, he explained, with completion by the following spring. Until then, Americana would stay open and operational.

ABOVE: The Big Boy mascot greets children. BELOW: Ben Marcus's first theater in Ripon, Wisconsin.

Creating a Destination

Steve Magnuson spent fifteen years as the general manager at Grand Geneva before moving on to a vice president position within the Marcus Corporation. He was in Lake Geneva from the moment Marcus acquired the Americana property, and closely monitored its renovation and expansion. "[At Marcus] we have a history of taking over properties that were either bankrupt or underperforming or in foreclosure," he points out, citing the Marcus Corporation's famous salvage of the historic Pfister Hotel in Milwaukee. "We have the ability to see the potential and keep the property profitable for the long-run. Some people come in and do what we call the lipstick-and-rouge renovation [with the intention of flipping the profit quickly]. But we have a mindset where we're long-term owners of an asset. We're willing to invest for the long-term and see the long-term potential and reward."

At Grand Geneva, this involved creating a resort that was appealing not just to casual tourists but to conferences and large groups as well. "It needed to become more of a meeting hotel as well as a leisure destination," Magnuson explains. "We needed to get more group businesses in there to be successful 365 days a year. We needed more centralized meeting space and a bigger ballroom. Secondly, we needed to create an experience of getting away, so we added destination restaurants. Also, there was no gathering place at the resort because it was all nooks and crannies when it was designed to be a couples place [during the Playboy days], but people increasingly wanted to gather in public spaces. Today, everyone wants to work in the lobbies. So we took out the indoor swimming pool, put in the lobby lounge as a gathering place and moved the front desk to make it a bigger, more attractive entrance."

That was just the beginning. In subsequent renovations, Marcus redesigned the two golf courses to make them more resort- and amateur-friendly, added a full-service spa (one of the first in the area, Magnuson points out), upgraded the ski hill and expanded the ski school, created six outdoor tennis courts, renovated the fitness center and upgraded the equipment, further expanded the meeting and conference facilities, and added a childcare center for hotel guests and employees.

During the fifteen years Magnuson lived in Lake Geneva, he served as the chairman of the Lake Geneva Area Convention and Visitors Bureau, working with local government and other businesses to establish local events that would benefit guests at Grand Geneva as well as residents of the area. Because of this collaboration, Grand Geneva hosts popular events such as "Christmas in the Country" — featuring an impressive winter light display and Christmas-themed theater — and Fourth of July fireworks. They also sponsor the annual snow-sculpting competition that is part of Lake Geneva's Winterfest every year. "[At Grand Geneva], we employ about 700 people year-round and about 1,000 during peak season," he says. "We always wanted to give back to the community. Marcus has always believed that businesses make up a community. It was all about coming together to bring even more people into the community."

When asked what he's most proud of about his time at Grand Geneva, Magnuson says, "I think it was just the fact that we were able to create a destination feeling... that we're able to create a sense of a place apart. We came up with a slogan: Minutes Away and Worlds Apart. We tried to create a place for our target market that was within a two-hour drive, but the people who came had the opportunity to experience something you don't get anywhere else in the Midwest. People fondly remember the Playboy Club-Hotel, but they always tell you, the Playboy Club-Hotel was never as good as Grand Geneva has become. People keep coming back, and have such great things to say."

Renovations to the old Americana lobby opened up the space, and a soaring, floor-to-ceiling fireplace was built. © Bill Frantz

A Property's Rebirth

Berthelsen had studied the business trends, seasonal vacation activity, and related tourism/hospitality conditions in the Lake Geneva area and felt the resort could thrive again. "It's the kind of experience that, when you drive through the gates, you don't hear phones ringing or horns honking," says Berthelsen. "This is one of the prettiest 1,300 acres of real estate in the entire state of Wisconsin." Steve Marcus agreed with Berthelsen that the resort "was a magnificent piece of property." He pointed out that the basic facilities were "outstanding, well thought out, very complete."

The sale of the Americana property was exciting for the Lake Geneva community because the Marcus Corporation was Milwaukee-based and well-regarded in the hospitality industry. The property that Marcus acquired included a private lake, a hotel with about 400 guest rooms, two golf courses, an airport, ski slopes, a 40,000-square foot convention center, four indoor tennis courts, five racquetball courts, two swimming pools, and a fitness center.

The resort was shuttered in the fall of 1993 as renovation commenced under the watchful eye of John Farmer, director of acquisitions and development for Marcus Hotels. The corporation invested around $30 million in the project, rebranding the resort Grand Geneva and repositioning the property as one of the premier resorts in the upper Midwest.

In addition to bringing prestige to the area, the renovation and re-opening of Grand Geneva also brought 500 jobs. "We really felt the loss of visitors and jobs when Americana closed," said then-Lake Geneva mayor Bea Dale, adding, "This is real positive for us."

Many previous employees of both the Playboy and the Americana years were eager to land jobs again at the complex. Marilyn Roth started as a seamstress for the Playboy Club-Hotel and lived only thirteen miles from the resort. After Playboy closed, Roth stayed on with Americana as administrative assistant to the complex's chief engineer. For twelve years, she watched as her workplace steadily fell apart and noted that twenty-some companies walked away from buying it. To Roth, it seemed that no one wanted the complex at any price due to the extent of needed repairs.

When Marcus bought the property, Roth was euphoric. "It was exciting to see it revived after watching it deteriorate," she says. Roth went on to assist the project manager during the renovation and stayed on in the engineering department from 1994 to 1996,

ABOVE: A grander, Prairie-style gateway was built at the resort's entrance. BELOW: The outdoor pool was renovated when Marcus purchased the property in 1993, and in 2009, the pool deck was expanded and water features were added. © Bill Frantz

when she was promoted to director of purchasing.

Steve Magnuson served as the General Manager at Grand Geneva for the first fifteen years. "There were key associates from Playboy and Americana both in management and hourly roles that either remained on or came back when Grand Geneva opened," he recalls. "They were a tremendous help in bridging the gap between the Playboy Club-Hotel and Grand Geneva. Even though the Playboy era ended in 1982, many guests remember it fondly. It was our strategy to not copy the Playboy Club-Hotel, but to build upon the amenities that defined the resort."

The Marcus renovation turned the decrepit complex into a state-of-the-art facility. The plans included a major reconfiguration of the interior that moved the registration desk, shifted the indoor pool, and created a lobby lounge and living room space. It also enhanced and updated the restaurants and lounge. Under the renovation, the former Briar Patch golf course was renamed The Highlands and was redesigned to play in four hours, rather than the previously vigorous six-hour stretch. The former recording studio space was turned into an engineering office and the air strip was recertified and reopened. The drive into the resort — christened the Cottontail Trail during the Playboy years — was renamed Grand Geneva Way, a perfect complement to the new motto "Minutes Away, Worlds Apart." A new entryway and signage welcomed visitors to the new Grand Geneva.

Convention space was increased to 50,000 square feet of meeting and exhibit space, and the sound, lighting, and telecommunications systems were updated. An 8,000-square-foot ballroom in the center of the building completed the convention space. The masculine environment of faux leather and polished metals dating from the old Playboy Club-Hotel was replaced by "the quiet, rustic elegance of an inviting family home in the country," according to Marcus internal communications at the time. Hefner's manly mystique gave way to an elegant "country home" image.

Former Grand Geneva Director of Sales and Marketing Dan Hoppe emphasized that the property was renovated "from top to bottom," and included an addition to the golf clubhouse and pro shop featuring a new fifty-seat bar and grill. The resort also added a daycare center to help attract large group meetings and families. The renovations made Grand Geneva's convention capacity the largest in Wisconsin.

The Frank Lloyd Wright Legacy

Wisconsin native Frank Lloyd Wright was a visionary who many around the world consider to be the greatest American architect. His designs stand tall over large cities such as Tokyo as well as smaller communities all over the world, where they function as houses of worship, libraries, museums, and residences.

Before Frank Lloyd Wright's influence, house design rarely strayed from the homogenous, boxy, Victorian-style. Wright pulled apart these confined floor plans, opened up spaces with tall windows, and centered the home around the hearth. Many of his creations populate the region, and his vision continues to live on in Wright-inspired designs on Geneva Lake and throughout the area.

The soft, rolling prairie on which Grand Geneva is built is the ideal setting for a Wright-inspired design. The hotel's original architects were influenced by the Prairie-style concept popularized by Frank Lloyd Wright. This style came about in the early 1900s and is characterized by long, low-style designs with open floor plans, a central chimney, overhanging eaves, rows of windows, and abstraction of form. This style is known as the first authentic American style of architecture, as it was a reaction to the monotonous European styles of its time, such as Neo-classical, Victorian, and Colonial.

After purchasing the property in 1993, resort renovators committed to preserving the original architectural style that both complemented and showcased its outside surroundings so well. The Prairie style of architecture is exemplified in Grand Geneva's inviting open-plan lobby; the earthy tones which match the outdoors and the tall windows overlooking the area's natural splendor. The low-lying structure is tucked into the rolling landscape.

In the summer of 2005, the resort completed changes to the

© Holly Leitner

new entryway and the exterior. The brick and wood walkway wraps around the building as if melding together exterior and interior worlds. Lining it are Wright-inspired abstract-designed light fixtures and an abundance of greenery surrounding the structure. The glass roof atop the grand entrance to the lobby allows natural light to pour in, and the repeated linear design of the new structure exemplifies Wright's belief that form must follow function.

Wright's designs continue to inspire new dwellings and destinations throughout the area. In addition, his legacy lives on through five authentic designs still standing on the shores of Delavan Lake and through stories of the lost Lake Geneva landmark, the Geneva Hotel.

As future enhancements are planned for the property, Grand Geneva meticulously preserves the Wright-influenced legacy of its original construction, and adds structures that blend seamlessly into the existing edifice, creating a building and grounds that are in themselves a work of art.

Before

After

Grand Geneva's suites, remodeled in 2009, feature expanded bathrooms with large Jacuzzi tubs, granite counter tops, and hardwood flooring.

A Commitment to Excellence

Since opening Grand Geneva in 1994, the Marcus Corporation has worked to further enhance the quality of the resort. They added three successful restaurants: Ristoranté Brissago, the Geneva ChopHouse, and the Grand Café. In addition to golfing and skiing, new recreation was added in 2001 in the form of the Timber Ridge Lodge & Waterpark, a 50,000-square-foot, indoor/outdoor water park. Horseback riding and a full-service spa were also added.

In 2006, a 12,000-square-foot conference center was added, expanding the resort's total square footage of banquet, meeting, and exhibit space to more than 60,000. The space was designed to accommodate groups of all sizes with the latest audio-visual technology available.

By 2009, major upgrades included expansion of the outdoor pool deck featuring eight arching fountains; a California-style fire pit and dining area adjacent to the Geneva ChopHouse; and enhancements to the resort's signature spa and salon. A complete remodel of all the guest rooms was completed with Seura television mirrors in all bathrooms, while suites featured gas fireplaces, LCD flat-screen televisions, wet bars with granite counter tops, and expanded bathrooms with large Jacuzzi tubs.

Grand Geneva plays a key role in the community, employing up to 1,000 people in peak season. Managers are active in many community organizations; some also serve on local government boards and committees. Among Grand Geneva's many community outreach activities are the resort's Annual Winter Coat Drive benefitting Clothing Outreach of Walworth County and a non-perishable food collection that benefits the Lake Geneva Area Food Pantry.

Under the ownership of the Marcus Corporation, Grand Geneva has earned a coveted AAA Four Diamond rating for more than 17 consecutive years. This rating is one of the most prestigious trademarks in the global travel industry. Other awards include *Condé Nast Traveler*'s Reader Poll for Top 10 Northern U.S. Golf Resorts, *Meetings and Convention*'s Gold Key Award; voted one of the Top 20 Family Resorts by *Celebrated Living Magazine*; *U.S. News & World Report*'s Top 10 Best Hotels in Wisconsin; *Smart Meetings* Platinum Choice Award; and *Meetings and Convention*'s Gold Tee Award.

The main entrance was dramatically remodeled in 2005.

What's in a Name?

Many of Grand Geneva's meeting rooms are named after original Geneva Lake estates.

Westgate. © Clint Farlinger

Westgate

Westgate was a vast, thirty-four-room English Tudor manor home, complete with a 164-foot-long basement for activities such as bowling and billiards. One of its later owners, Marie Pisor, created an amazing dollhouse reproduction that is now on display at the Webster House Museum in Elkhorn. The home was torn down in 2008.

Swinghurst

Chicago preacher David Swing found a retreat from urban life at Swinghurst. The home included exterior and interior balconies where Swing could deliver his sermons. He also had a large, sunken tub installed

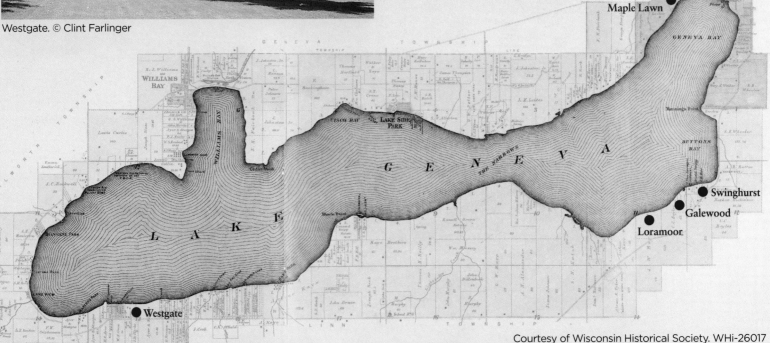

Courtesy of Wisconsin Historical Society. WHi-26017

Swinghurst. Photo courtesy of Lake Geneva Public Library

Loramoor. Photo courtesy of Lake Geneva Public Library

Maple Lawn. Courtesy of Wisconsin Historical Society. WHi-36471

Galewood. Photo courtesy of Lake Geneva Public Library

on the first floor where he regularly baptized members of his flock. The estate still stands today.

Maple Lawn

Maple Lawn is attributed to architect Henry Lord Gay. Built in 1871 for Chicago banker Shelton Sturges, the mansion boasted a five-story square tower. By the end of its life, the home was believed to have spanned 12,000 square feet, with a dozen bedrooms and bathrooms. It was razed in 2005.

Loramoor

Built in 1900 by James H. Moore, whose ventures include what we now know as Nabisco, Loramoor was one of the grandest estates to grace the lake. All that remains is a handful of its original thirty-two outbuildings, including the horse stable and gatehouse, which are both now private homes.

Galewood

Built in 1893, the original home was destroyed by fire in 1928, and the home that was built in its place is known as Casa del Sueño. It was once owned by Lee Phillip Bell and Bill Bell, creators of the soap opera "The Young and the Restless." They named the show's town after nearby Genoa City.

Today, the Grand Geneva property comprises approximately 1,300 acres just east of Lake Geneva. As the story goes, the large, 22-acre manmade lake created by Playboy was designed in the shape of a bunny head. One of the smaller lakes was designed in the shape of a heart. Both lakes are stocked with fish.

Grand Geneva — A Timeless Resort

THE RESORT COMBINES AN ENCHANTING LANDSCAPE WITH AWARD-WINNING AMENITIES

SINCE OPENING IN 1994, Grand Geneva's management has continued to add amenities and enhancements to its property on an ongoing basis. Today the resort has 355 guest rooms and suites, two golf courses, a spa and fitness center, meeting and convention facilities, a ski hill, several restaurants and an airport. As the Lake Geneva area continues to be recognized as a top Midwestern vacation destination, Grand Geneva provides award-winning resort facilities for visitors from across the nation and worldwide.

One of the more recent additions to the resort is the Geneva Club, a private lounge located on the main level. The exclusive access to the Geneva Club allows guests to enjoy the quiet lounge atmosphere, which includes a fireplace, comfortable casual seating with reading materials, dining area, games, and workstations for individuals or small business groups. Wi-Fi Internet access, printers, and televisions are also available.

The Geneva Club complements the overall experience at Grand Geneva, as a place to unwind after a round of golf, visit to the fitness center, or as a gathering place before dinner at one of the resort's restaurants.

Award-Winning Golf

Since the grand opening of the Playboy Club-Hotel in 1968, the resort has offered top-notch golfing options. The Robert Bruce Harris-designed Brute, an 18-hole, PGA-caliber golf course, measures more than 7,000 yards and is marked by elevated greens, sixty-eight sand traps and water hazards on nine holes. Harris embraced practical, simplified design, demonstrated by sand traps, which he insisted should be designed so the grass on their slopes could be maintained by fairway mowers.

When the course was completed at an astonishing cost of $1.8 million, Harris said, "I've tried to design it so it will be a pleasure for all classes of players. I think it's going to work out to be about the most beautiful course in America. But I am a modest man, and I would like to have golfers give their evaluation."

While The Brute was carefully carved out of the surrounding countryside, the resort's second course, The Briar Patch, was designed around the natural lay of the land by Pete Dye and a young Jack Nicklaus, who wanted to leave the landscape as natural as possible to create a Scottish-style course. Nicklaus was at the height of his career when he was brought in as a consultant in 1967, having won the Masters Tournament in 1965 and 1966; he would go on to win his second US Open in 1970. The two courses proved to be extremely popular with visitors, drawing celebrities and professional golfers as well as resort guests and local duffers.

Bill Pullen, managing director of the Playboy Club-Hotel from 1970 to 1972, remembers the weekend the resort hosted the first annual Brian Piccolo pro-am tournament: "We had so many of the principal sports stars of the Midwest there." According to David Hallenbeck, Grand Geneva's golf director since the 1970s, the two golf courses at Grand Geneva have hosted a lengthy roster of celebrities and famous athletes over the years: Bart Starr, Arnold Palmer, Robin Yount, Paul Molitor, Mickey Mantle, Mike Ditka, Reggie White, Brett Favre, Stan Makita, Lee Trevino, Gary Player, Bob Hope, Joe Walsh, and John Denver, among many, many others.

After taking over the resort in 1993, the Marcus Corporation invested heavily in refreshing the courses. Steve Magnuson, general manager of Grand Geneva from 1993 to 2008, said the links were badly in need of a little attention: "We put a lot of money into the golf courses, to make them worthy of their heritage."

Beginning in 1995, The Briar Patch underwent a major renovation by noted golf architect Bob Cupp, at which time it was renamed The Highlands. "We felt The Briar Patch wasn't a resort-friendly golf course at that time," explains Magnuson. "It had a lot of trick shots and blind shots. We wanted it to

CONTINUED ON PAGE 93

The Brute

The Highlands

Weddings at Grand Geneva

COUPLES CHOOSE GRAND GENEVA FOR ITS BEAUTY AND EASE OF PLANNING

From the rehearsal dinner to official wedding ceremony, reception, and romantic honeymoon, Grand Geneva helps couples plan the perfect wedding celebration. The resort's grounds are an ideal backdrop for photos. Guests find plenty to do, from a round of golf to relaxing at the pool or spa, to a trail ride on horseback. And with so many on-site activities available, couples don't need to leave the resort until the honeymoon is over.

CONTINUED FROM PAGE 88

be more amateur-friendly and female-friendly to attract travel golfers." The updated facilities included a modernized pro shop with high-end merchandise, a driving range, and a Golf Learning Center. Further renovations to the course followed in 2006, completed by Bob Lohmann.

According to Magnuson, The Brute and The Highlands are frequently listed among the top 10 golf courses in Wisconsin, and in 2012, Grand Geneva was selected by a *Condé Nast Traveler* reader's poll as one of the top ten golf resorts in the northern United States. Hallenbeck attributes the courses' continued popularity to the Marcus Corporation's excellent stewardship: "It's not just the wonderful courses that make golfing here special," he says. "There's the history of this place and prestige that comes with being a Four Diamond resort."

A Day at the Spa

When the Playboy Club-Hotel opened in 1968, tennis and racquet sports were extremely popular, so the resort plans included the Lake Geneva Fitness and Racquet Centre, a freestanding structure near the main building. The courts were a popular diversion for guests throughout the 1970s and into the early 1980s, and even hosted celebrities and well-known athletes.

As guests' tastes evolved throughout the decades, however, the Fitness and Racquet Centre began to seem outdated. When the Marcus Corporation bought the property in 1993, their renovation plans included the addition of one of the area's first full-service spas. "Back then, when I said we were building a 'spa,' people thought we were adding one whirlpool," remembers Magnuson.

"When we took over the property, we created the spa and sports center," he continues. "We were one of the first real destination spas in the Midwest." The new spa and fitness center added square footage so that the pool could be moved from the main building into the fitness center and be upgraded to a Junior Olympic size. The expanded building also allowed for the introduction of additional fitness equipment and provided space for a full menu of newly popular spa amenities like massages, facials, and salon services.

The new destination spa was such a success that another expansion soon followed, including a renovation of the tennis courts. The 42,000-square-foot WELL Spa + Salon is a major draw for resort guests. The fitness center offers the lap pool, whirlpools, steam rooms, a fitness studio, an indoor climbing wall, all the latest fitness equipment, and courts for basketball, volleyball, and tennis. A full schedule of fitness classes are offered weekly. In the spa, guests can take advantage of a wide range of services from massages

CONTINUED ON PAGE 96

Christmas in the Country

WISCONSIN'S WINTER WONDERLAND COMES TO LIFE

Since 1996, Grand Geneva has maximized its location in the beautiful Wisconsin winter landscape by turning the 1,300-acre resort into a dazzling winter wonderland of special holiday activities. The events, which range from fireworks and a spectacular holiday light display to Christmas caroling and brunch with Santa, are known collectively as Christmas in the Country. From Thanksgiving through New Year's, Grand Geneva fulfills visitors' cultural yearning for a relaxing, bucolic holiday experience.

Christmas in the Country began as a partnership between the Marcus Corporation and the Lake Geneva Area Convention and Visitors Bureau (LGCVB) as a way to entice travelers to the Lake Geneva area during the off-season. Former General Manager Steve Magnuson also served on the board of the LGCVB, eventually serving as its president. He says one of the issues that the city of Lake Geneva was grappling with at the time was the decline in tourism during the winter. "[Christmas in the Country was] the biggest initiative we ever did," he says. "We created that initiative to help fill the year from November through New Year's. We wanted to create an event about lights, food, and entertainment that would draw people to Lake Geneva."

Each year, the festivities kick off with the Illumination Ceremony, which features the lighting of two million lights across the resort's property. An elaborate fireworks display follows. "That was also a great way for us to connect with the community," Magnuson says. "We got a lot of local interest in our fireworks and the light displays, and we made that available to the community free of charge." Magnuson says that spirit of community collaboration is part of the Marcus Corporation's philosophy: "We always wanted to give back to the community. Marcus has always believed that businesses make up a community and the community supports your business."

Other Christmas in the Country activities include Christmas-themed theater, a gingerbread house competition, brunch with Santa, Christmas caroling, traditional afternoon teas, and special dining events. Now an annual tradition, Christmas in the Country draws a steady stream of visitors to the area throughout the holiday season and has proven to be a popular attraction for local residents as well.

CONTINUED FROM PAGE 93

and facials to aromatherapy and body treatments, manicures, and pedicures. In addition to these amenities, wellness retreats are offered periodically, engaging guests in fitness, nutrition, and mind/body classes as well.

Hitting the Trail

Dan Patch Stables is named for the famed turn-of-the-century racehorse who spent part of his retirement living in Lake Geneva in the stable of Chicago banker John J. Mitchell. Dan Patch Stables offers guided trail rides, pony rides, and carriage rides around the resort grounds. In autumn, families enjoy a Haunted Hayride. In snowy weather, experience a horse-drawn sleigh ride. Guests with children can visit the free petting farm that includes a variety of barnyard animals.

Ski Season

Skiing was a part of the winter Playboy Club-Hotel experience from the earliest days of the resort. In fact, even before Playboy developed the land east of Lake Geneva, the spot was home to a small ski hill called Indian Knob. The original Playboy Club-Hotel ski area consisted of two hills: a bunny slope (the play-on-words must have been irresistible to the ski area's designers) and a hill for more advanced skiers, each of which had a chair lift.

Initially the ski area was reserved solely for the use of hotel guests, but in 1971, the slopes were opened to the public, and the resort contracted with the Ray T. Stemper ski school to provide lessons to beginners. This proved to be an extremely popular decision, drawing skiers from throughout the local area. "If I had a dime for everyone who told me they learned how to ski on those hills…" says Steve Magnuson with a laugh.

Peter Adam Crook, a former resident of Lake Geneva, learned to ski at the Mountain Top while in grade school. He continued skiing there through the start of high school and then moved to Colorado to attend the Vail Ski and Snowboard Academy. He represented the British Virgin Islands, where his family now lives, in the 2014 Winter Olympics in Sochi, Russia, competing in the Men's Half-pipe Final event.

According to Hans Hauschild, Grand Geneva's former ski director and a staff member since the Playboy days, the Playboy Club-Hotel expanded the slopes in 1976 by adding an additional chairlift accessing new expert and intermediate terrain. The new expert terrain was called "Hotdog Mountain." The beginner teaching area was also expanded by installing two rope tows at that same time.

When Americana bought the property in 1981, the recently updated ski slopes continued to attract visitors, particularly day-pass and season-pass skiers, even as the resort itself fell into disrepair. "By the end of Americana's

tenure at the resort, I think only the golf courses and the ski hill were still making money," remembers Magnuson.

After the Marcus Corporation took over the resort, they invested in updates to the ski area. "We wanted to attract even more day-pass and season-pass skiers," Magnuson explains. To this end, they removed the rope tows and installed "Magic Carpet" lifts, upgraded all of the ski rental equipment, and hired a staff of eighty ski instructors. The ski chalet, originally designed by Alexander McIlvaine to resemble two intersecting snowflakes, was expanded in 2002.

Today the ski area, known as The Mountain Top, features three chairlifts, two conveyor lifts, and eighteen slopes ranging from beginner areas to expert courses. There's a terrain park for skiers and snowboarders and more than twenty snowmaking machines to ensure powder even in the driest winters. The resort hosts a celebration of winter activities in February each year with a Winter Carnival, which includes snowboard competitions, slalom races, a torchlight parade, and fireworks display. For over a decade, The Mountain Top has also hosted the Snocross National Championships, featuring racers who also compete in the Winter X-Games.

Timber Ridge Lodge & Waterpark

When the Marcus Corporation took over Grand Geneva, the company's initial priorities involved restoration and renovation of the properties' existing amenities. But by 2000, the resort was so successful that Marcus decided to invest in a significant addition. Capitalizing on the rising popularity of indoor water parks in other Wisconsin resort locations, Marcus announced an ambitious expansion plan: Timber Ridge Lodge & Waterpark.

The new water park hotel was constructed south of the main building and fitness center, and contains a 30,000-square-foot indoor water park and a 20,000-square-foot outdoor water play area. A total of 225 one- and two-bedroom suites were also added as a part of the new space. They offer amenities like full kitchens, living areas, covered balconies, and fireplaces.

Timber Ridge opened in July of 2001 and has proved to be extremely popular. The indoor water park contains Timber Rapids and Avalanche Falls, two large water slides rising more than thirty feet into the air. It also contains a lazy river, an in-water basketball court, multiple hot tubs, play areas for smaller children, and a snack bar.

Smokey's Bar-B-Que House, the first barbecue restaurant in the Lake Geneva area, was added to serve guests at Timber Ridge Lodge. It is designed to resemble an old Wisconsin logging camp.

Geneva ChopHouse

Smokey's Bar-B-Que House at Timber Ridge Lodge

Steve Magnuson credits Timber Ridge with the continued success of the resort. "That's what it takes to be successful: taking a long-term look and finding ways to make the resort popular year-round. The water park adds another amenity that creates year-round demand."

Savor the Moment

The Playboy Club-Hotel was famous for its elegant dining options. The VIP Room, Playboy's top-of-the-line dining room, earned a national reputation for excellence. The Living Room Restaurant, a buffet-style dining room designed to resemble a medieval hunting lodge, and the Playmate Bar offered more casual fare but still exuded an ambiance of exclusivity. Playboy's dining options were designed to provide privacy and intimacy to the resort's target demographic: couples.

When Americana took over the resort, they sought to renovate the dining rooms to make them more family-friendly. The Living Room Restaurant became Annie's Country Kitchen, and the Playmate Bar was converted to the Steakhouse and Saloon.

By the time the Marcus Corporation took over the property, the restaurants (like the rest of the property) were badly in need of updating. "One of the things we wanted to do when we took over the property was to create a destination experience," explains Magnuson. "Somewhere people could escape to and feel like they were miles away from their regular lives. We needed to go after that experience, so we created destination restaurants."

The Marcus Corporation initially added three newly renovated restaurants: the Newport Grill, Ristoranté Brissago, and the Grand Café. Subsequent renovations converted the Newport Grill into the Geneva ChopHouse and added additional dining options, including Smokey's Bar-B-Que House and the Hungry Moose food court at Timber Ridge Lodge.

Today, the Geneva ChopHouse is a top-rated steak and seafood restaurant that boasts a menu of over ninety different wines. It features an outdoor cocktail lounge called Embers Terrace, where live entertainment is available on weekend nights throughout the summer.

Named after a small town in northern Italy on Lake Maggiori, Ristoranté Brissago features a menu that rivals most big-city Italian-style restaurants. Several menu items feature handmade pasta, and the restaurant also boasts a carefully curated list of Italian wines, expertly paired by restaurant staff.

Adjacent to the Lobby Lounge, the Grand Café offers a warm ambiance for breakfast, lunch, and dinner with sweeping views of the resort property. The contemporary cuisine menu is designed to appeal to a wide variety of palates.

Ristoranté Brissago

For guests who are busy taking advantage of the resort's many amenities, food and beverage options are available on site. At the Golf Shop, the Links Bar and Grill serves up casual fare along with beer and cocktails for before or after tee time. The Mountain Top Lodge is open during ski season for warm-ups and après-ski dining. And in the main lobby, Café Gelato serves up coffee and specialty drinks on the go.

A Little Nightlife

A nightcap, live jazz, or dancing are all just a short stroll away. Relax into the evening with a variety of entertainment options. Enjoy live musicians nightly in the lobby lounge. Savor the outdoors while indulging in a delectable dessert fireside at Embers Terrace. Or get into the groove of a live DJ at Evolve, Grand Geneva's stylish nightclub.

Think of the lobby lounge as an oversized living room, with a massive fireplace and views of the outdoor pool deck. Nearly every evening you can enjoy live music from a pianist, guitarist, or jazz trio as you enjoy a glass of wine or cocktail from the lobby bar. It's the perfect place for conversation and relaxation after a busy day.

For an alfresco nighttime experience, save room for dessert and an after-dinner drink at Embers Terrace, Geneva ChopHouse's outdoor cocktail lounge. At Embers Terrace, guests can enjoy sweet treats while cozying up to the outdoor fireplace. Live entertainment is often scheduled under the stars on summer weekends.

Evolve is another popular night spot at Grand Geneva, with plush seating groups that are perfect for gathering with friends or meeting up after a day's work. Evolve features a creative martini menu along with small plate appetizers and desserts, a full bar with a wide selection of drink options, and specialty cocktails. A live DJ gets the dance floor going several nights a week.

The Next Chapter

This 1,300-acre property that began under the Playboy name in 1968 has welcomed generations of guests in its nearly five decades as an iconic Midwestern resort. From its humble beginnings to today's luxurious amenities, Grand Geneva's chapter is far from over.

Each year, as more and more new brides and grooms celebrate their weddings here, new traditions are established as they return for anniversaries and later, begin lifelong family traditions of staying and playing at Grand Geneva. We look forward to being the destination for these traditions, events, and celebrations for years to come.

The Links Bar and Grill

The Lobby Lounge

Memories

RESORT GUESTS AND EMPLOYEES SHARE THEIR FAVORITE ANECDOTES AND EXPERIENCES

DURING THE DEVELOPMENT OF THIS BOOK, the editors asked resort guests and employees to send in their favorite memories of this property. Here is just a sampling of the many responses that were received.

"Our family loved coming to Lake Geneva; I have so many great memories. The [Playboy] Club-Hotel was such a comfortable place. We loved the outdoor activities — we had a pony there, so we were there all the time. In fact, my sister was almost named Geneva, because my Dad was working there when my mom went into labor with her.

I opened a restaurant in Evanston in October 2012, and I had to put a French dip sandwich on the menu because it reminded me of the Lake Geneva Playboy Club-Hotel. It was one of their most popular."

—Amy Morton, Daughter of Arnold (Arnie) Morton

I have been fortunate to have many wonderful memories of my years with the resort. Before chair lift A was installed, we had a heated swimming pool at the ski area. After the lifts closed for the night we occasionally would go swimming and then go to the upstairs bar to talk and laugh with other ski hill staff, area employees, and of course the Playboy bunnies. But my very favorite memory was meeting my wife for the first time while riding on the current "B" chair lift in 1982. She was and still is a ski instructor.

—Erik Bayer, Volunteer Ski Patrol

I have been coming up to Grand Geneva since I was eleven years old, when it was the Playboy Club-Hotel. My most memorable moment was seeing the Jackson 5 walk through the lobby. Michael Jackson had to be ten or eleven years old as well. My family and I continue to visit the Grand often and love it. The best experience was watching my son ski for the first time with his dad!

—Charise Rossi, Guest

We spent our honeymoon at the Playboy Club-Hotel, in July 1968. We were on a budget back then and our dream was to go to Jamaica. We decided on the Playboy Club-Hotel in Lake Geneva instead. It was brand new then. We chose a "parking lot" view as the room rate was a few dollars cheaper than Lakeview. I believe the rates were $22 and $26, respectively. We didn't do much looking out of the window anyway. We retired early when we heard someone trying to get into our room. We were startled, and it was the maid, who was coming in to turn down the bed and leave mints on our pillows.

—Susan Hayunga, Guest

My 15 years with Playboy were some of the best times in my life. The company was incredible to work for, and as I always say, I received an education no one could ever pay for!

—Gail Hintz Frantz, Bunny Mother

My family purchased a timeshare at the Playboy Club-Hotel in 1976 in White River Village. In those early days, the hotel had a special game room for family members to enjoy, and you could win Playboy memorabilia as prizes. My six-year-old son just loved it.

That winter, I received a call from my son's teacher who was very amused at his essay on how he spent his Christmas holiday, which he entitled "Playing Backgammon with the Bunnies." I was a little embarrassed, but did admit that it was absolutely true and that he did indeed play Backgammon with one of the Playboy bunnies in the hotel's game room. To this day, I still have that handwritten story, and my son is now an adult with a child of his own. Retelling this story still makes me smile.

—Constance Neven, Guest

George and Barbara Bush were here and I arranged a dinner that they were guests at, and on the order I put "Chef's Choice" for vegetable and Chef did broccoli — George hates broccoli! He thought it was a joke; when served he said, "Very funny." He was a good sport and just didn't eat it.

—Jerry Fenner, Events staff

We had our wedding reception in the Grand Ballroom in November 1994. We were the first big event after all of the remodeling and reopening as Grand Geneva. I think we had around 300 guests. It was decorated beautifully and we had an amazing time. Everyone there told us it was the best wedding reception they'd ever been to. A night I will never forget!

—Brooke Grunow, Guest

"I performed at the Lake Geneva Playboy Club-Hotel for the first time in 1969 and it was glorious — a great club that was always packed. I didn't go back until the mid-1970s, and by then the crowds were smaller, which I attributed to the rock bands they were booking. Playboy had always been synonymous with jazz. Sam Distenfano and Carlos Cicirello asked me if I would go to Chicago to meet Mr. Hefner and Victor Lownes to discuss my ideas. I agreed and was hired to open "Lainie's Room West" at the Playboy Club in L.A., and a few years later I opened "Lainie's Room East" at the Playboy Club in New York City.

—Lainie Kazan, Jazz Performer and Actress

We lived in the Town of Lyons for thirty years. I remember when the hotel and grounds were purchased, fell apart, and then became Grand Geneva. The property has taken on such a beautiful look, be it spring, summer, fall, or winter. We loved riding through the front gate, seeing all of the flowers, and the Christmas lights. We always stopped in for lunch. We just thank the people who work at Grand Geneva for being so nice, all the time. We visit four times a year, for the changing of each season.

—Georgette Lee, Guest

We started going to Timber Ridge four years ago for Christmas in the Country with my then almost-two-year-old. Now it is a yearly tradition. We love the water park, seeing all of the holiday decorations, and having breakfast with Santa. He's almost six and his brother is now three. It's amazing to see how much they've grown year to year. The older one was finally able to try the big water slide this year! I love our yearly trip; it's become so much of a tradition that I can't imagine the holidays without it.

—Melissa Rubik, Guest

My favorite memory from Grand Geneva takes place most summer weekends when I take my friends to Evolve and the outdoor firepit. Whenever I have friends in from out of town, they always want something that resembles a Chicago nightlife scene. A place where they can get delicious drinks and have the possibility of making new friends. This place never fails. It is my number one spot in Lake Geneva in the summer to make new friends and chit chat with a perfect size appetizer. My out-of-town friends love it and my local friends love it. Keep making great memories for both visitors and locals.

—Sophia Erzumiah, Guest

I used to visit as a teen in the late 1980s when it was the Americana, to play laser tag and to hang out at the recording studio. I sat through the entire "18 & Life" recording for Skid Row! We used to hang out at the pool and have a lot of fun. We stayed in room 307 and went to all of the concerts at Alpine Valley.

—Barbara Wells, Guest

If someone were to ask me what I enjoyed most about being a Playboy bunny back in the '70s, I think I would say the diversity within my job. Some Sunday mornings I'd teach backgammon in the Game Room. I'll never forget getting beat by a 10-year-old student. Seasonally I would work at the pool, and the Pro Shop, the main dining room, The Cabaret with the entertainers and lots of private parties. Every day was different.

I remember learning self-discipline early on. Every day we were written up on our performance and appearance. Gail, our "Bunny Mother," would inspect our shoes, uniforms, and make-up including false eyelashes. Every Saturday I remember weighing in. It was tough going through the daily process to look glamorous.

What I learned from that experience is that people are just people. We're basically all the same with different wants and needs, some with more opportunities. I have fond memories of being a bunny.

—Pam Ellis, Bunny

About ten years ago I won a radio contest in Chicago, and a weekend stay at Grand Geneva was the prize. I loved everything about the resort, and continued to go after winning the certificate. I started to buy gift cards because in 2006 I was getting married, and I wanted to surprise my husband by paying for our honeymoon. Well, it was perfect. The staff upgraded us to a suite. When I booked dinner at the ChopHouse we were given champagne and strawberries. We had dinner at Brissago and they gave us a dessert with a decorated plate and had roses on the table. I thought we were something special. We came back the following two years and it was just as good as ever. We are planning to return this year and I am so excited!

—Athena and John Clifford, Guests

Working as a bunny at The Playboy Club-Hotel in Lake Geneva was definitely a unique experience. Everything from the iconic costumes to meeting celebrities and developing a bond with other bunnies contributed to the fun and glamour.

—Kim Riba, Bunny

I have nearly two decades of favorite memories. Although we've stayed at Grand Geneva during different times of the year, I have to say that it's Christmas in the Country that's my favorite. My husband and I started coming the weekend after Thanksgiving when we were just dating. That didn't change once we were married, and then when our son was born, it just made it more special. We started to call it "The Christmas Hotel" because we told him that this is where Santa stays when he's not at the North Pole and that the Polar Express even stops there. Even now that my son is nine years old, he still insists we call it the Christmas Hotel, no matter what time of year we visit.

—Susan Molley, Guest

"When [Playboy] came, Lake Geneva no longer was just a place to sail your boat."

—George Hennerley, Former President, Lake Geneva Area Convention and Visitors Bureau

In the late '60s, my family moved to Lake Geneva from New Orleans because my father got a job with the Playboy Club-Hotel. His name was Paul Cruz but was often referred to as "Pablo" by his colleagues and guests of the Club. Due to his job, he often wore a tuxedo or white dinner jacket, and would spend inordinate amounts of time at home shining his shoes and his cuff links. I remember being so impressed with how handsome he looked as he left for work. The Playboy Club-Hotel was surely a glamorous place to be if he could look like Prince Charming through the eyes of a little girl. I used to pester him to get me a job at the Playboy Club-Hotel so I could be a part of this glittering world where he worked. But he always told me that I was much too young to work there. Someday, he always said. Someday.

One day, he needed to stop at work to pick something up and asked me if I wanted to go with him. I was so excited I could barely contain myself. He made me promise that if I was a good little girl, I might be able to see a real Playboy bunny. As we walked through the doors to the resort, I was struck by the most amazing sights! An indoor pool where you could swim from inside to outside — a river running through the hallway with little wooden bridges — it was all too much to take in. As I held my Dad's hand, we walked into the lounge where he worked and he propped me up on the bar. There I was surrounded by the most beautiful women I had ever seen (except for my Mom) and they were

all bunnies! I told them that when I grew up, I wanted to be a bunny too. Of course, they all laughed and told me that it would be a long time before I was able to work at the resort. My father smiled and said, "Someday."

It turned out to be many years later that I finally realized my dream to work at the Playboy Club-Hotel. In 2012, although what was once the Playboy Club-Hotel had long since been purchased by Marcus Corporation, I walked through those same doors to the resort that I once walked hand in hand with my father, and started my first day of work as the Director of Grand Experiences. Someday had finally come.

—Vicki Jacobs, Assistant Director of Operations

The memories that I have are very close to my heart. Working as a Playboy bunny was an adventure and an experience. It's hard to express the feelings you have of working in that era – how do you explain it? It was magical. One of my fondest memories was being a new bunny and going through training and learning how to do the bunny dip without falling off my high heels. I started working at this property several decades ago and I'm still here today.

—Pegs Weber, Bunny

Experiencing Grand Geneva as a local resident has been a part of my life since it opened. We've celebrated anniversaries and birthdays at the restaurants, viewed fireworks during Christmas in the Country and July 4th, and enjoyed the pools and water park as weekend guests with our children. Last February we stayed at the resort to watch the Academy Awards: we ordered room service, predicted the winners, and enjoyed our mini-vacation.

—Barb Krause, Guest

I enjoy arriving every day to work and being thankful for the beautiful views I get to take in. I love that I have gotten to experience so many of our events at the resort with my family, everything from 4th of July to Winter Carnival to the Illumination Ceremony and of course the water park, even though I am pretty sure my kids think I just swim in the water park all day. From the day I started working at the resort, I have heard so many stories from associates and past guests about back when it was the Playboy Club-Hotel. I am so happy we were able to gather up all of those great stories and the rich history of the property and put it in a book for all to enjoy.

—Courtney Nobilio, Director of Marketing Communications

Thank You

A *GRAND TALE* IS MADE POSSIBLE THROUGH OUR MANY CONTRIBUTORS

AS WITH ANY HISTORICAL PROJECT, there was no simple way to tell our story that spans more than forty-five years. Only by asking new questions, tapping new resources, and searching for fresh perspectives could we tell this fascinating tale. We'd like to express our sincere thanks to those who have helped us with our research and writing, including all of our past guests who submitted photos, stories, and memorabilia. And without the help of the many individuals, organizations, and historians listed below, we would have no story to share.

Jim Bartz	Jim Engel	Bill and Vikki LaCroix	Judy Roberts
Erik Bayer	Ron Fajerstein	Tish Lux	Richard Rosenzweig
Adrian Belew	Sandy Farwell	Steve Magnuson	Marilyn Roth
Rick Bolger	Bill and Gail Frantz	Leo Marubio	Larry Schroeder
Tom Burrows	Dave Hallenbeck	Don McElfresch	Dan Stone
Robert Butschke	George and Joan Hansen	Charles Moelter	Teri Thomerson
Bun E. Carlos	Susan Rapach Hayunga	Pat Moorhouse	Judy Thompson
Bea Dale	Christie Hefner	The family of	Greg Tipps
Rich Denhart	George Hennerley	Arnold Morton	Jim Uick
Sam and	John Himmel	Jerry Pawlak	Andy Waterman
Michael Distefano	Dan Hoppe	Ed Peller	Pegs Weber
Pam Ellis	Julie Ieronimo	Bill Pullen	

If you have stories or memorabilia you'd like to share, please call us at 800-558-3417.

References

ARCHIVES

Beloit Daily News
The Business Journal-Milwaukee
Chicago Tribune
Employee Handbook, Playboy Clubs and Playboy Club-Hotels, 1968
Golf Wisconsin
Inland Architect
Janesville Gazette
Lake Geneva Regional News
Lyons Township Historical Society
The Milwaukee Journal
Milwaukee Journal Sentinel
The Milwaukee Sentinel
Playboy Bunny Manual, Lake Geneva, 1968
Playboy Club Magazine
Playboy Club-Hotel Cottontails Newsletters, 1969-1970
Playboy Club-Hotel Hare's Herald Newsletters, 1972-1981
Playboy Magazine
Wisconsin Holiday News

ARTICLES AND BOOKS

Bennun, Dave, "Victor Lownes," *Stuff* Magazine, UK edition, 1998.

Eisile, Albert, "Someday, My Friend LeRoy Neiman Will Be Remembered As a Quintessential American Artist," *Minnesota Post*, 2012.

Dow, Janet, "The Blue Light: District/Unit News," *Chicago Police Star Magazine*, June 1969, June 1970, September 1971.

Lewis Line advertisement, Golfdom, October-November, 1969, p. 69.

Mueller, Art, *Progress Report on the Beautiful New Playboy Club - Hotel Course in Lake Geneva, Wisconsin.* Chicago: Art Mueller, 1968.

Saxon, Wolfgang, "Derick J. Daniels, 76, President of Playboy Empire in the 1970s, Dies," *New York Times*, 2005.

Spiro, Josh, "The Great Leaders Series: Hugh Hefner, Founder of Playboy Enterprises," Inc., February 2010.

"Tom Burrows," Lewis Line Catalog, 1970.

SPECIAL THANKS TO:

Lake Geneva Public Library
Geneva Lake Museum
Playboy Enterprises